THE UPPER ROOM

WHERE THE WORLD MEETS TO PRAY

Susan Hibbins
UK Editor

INTERDENOMINATIONAL
INTERNATIONAL
INTERRACIAL

33 LANGUAGES
Multiple formats are available in some languages

The Bible Reading Fellowship
15 The Chambers, Vineyard
Abingdon OX14 3FE
brf.org.uk

The Bible Reading Fellowship (BRF) is a Registered Charity (233280)

ISBN 978 0 85746 914 4
All rights reserved

Originally published in the USA by The Upper Room®
US edition © The Upper Room®
This edition © The Bible Reading Fellowship 2019
Cover image © Thinkstock

Acknowledgements

Scripture quotations marked NRSV are taken from The New Revised Standard Version of the Bible, Anglicised Edition, copyright © 1989, 1995 by the Division of Christian Education of the National Council of the Churches of Christ in the USA. Used by permission. All rights reserved.

Scripture quotations marked NIV are taken from The Holy Bible, New International Version (Anglicised edition) copyright © 1979, 1984, 2011 by Biblica. Used by permission of Hodder & Stoughton Publishers, an Hachette UK company. All rights reserved. 'NIV' is a registered trademark of Biblica. UK trademark number 1448790.

Extracts marked CEB are copyright © 2011 by Common English Bible.

Extracts marked KJV are taken from the Authorised Version of the Bible (The King James Bible), the rights in which are vested in the Crown, are reproduced by permission of the Crown's Patentee, Cambridge University Press.

Printed by Gutenberg Press, Tarxien, Malta

How to use *The Upper Room*

The Upper Room is ideal in helping us spend a quiet time with God each day. Each daily entry is based on a passage of scripture, and is followed by a meditation and prayer. Each person who contributes a meditation to the magazine seeks to relate their experience of God in a way that will help those who use *The Upper Room* every day.

Here are some guidelines to help you make best use of *The Upper Room*:

1 Read the passage of scripture. It is a good idea to read it more than once, in order to have a fuller understanding of what it is about and what you can learn from it.
2 Read the meditation. How does it relate to your own experience? Can you identify with what the writer has outlined from their own experience or understanding?
3 Pray the written prayer. Think about how you can use it to relate to people you know, or situations that need your prayers today.
4 Think about the contributor who has written the meditation. Some users of the *The Upper Room* include this person in their prayers for the day.
5 Meditate on the 'Thought for the day' and the 'Prayer focus', perhaps using them again as the focus for prayer or direction for action.

Why is it important to have a daily quiet time? Many people will agree that it is the best way of keeping in touch every day with the God who sustains us, and who sends us out to do his will and show his love to the people we encounter each day. Meeting with God in this way reassures us of his presence with us, helps us to discern his will for us and makes us part of his worldwide family of Christian people through our prayers.

I hope that you will be encouraged as you use the magazine regularly as part of your daily devotions, and that God will richly bless you as you read his word and seek to learn more about him.

Susan Hibbins
UK Editor

CAN YOU HELP?

Here at BRF, we're always looking for ways to promote the practice of daily Bible reading, and we would like to ask for your help in spreading the word about this valuable resource.

Can I ask you to spread the word about the usefulness of *The Upper Room* in aiding daily meditation and prayer? This could be among your friends and contacts, or at any events in which you might be involved, such as church or a Bible study group, or a conference, special service, retreat or workshop.

We would really value your help, and we'll happily send you some sample copies if you can use them. Just let me know how many you would like and I'll arrange for them to be sent to you. If you wish you can email me at **susan. hibbins@brf.org.uk**.

If you're active on social media, we can supply cover graphics for use on Twitter, Facebook and so on, and we can also supply information packs to churches and groups if you pass on any requests to me.

Thank you in advance for helping us to publicise our Bible reading notes.

Susan Hibbins
UK Editor, The Upper Room

Holding on to hope

Hope does not disappoint us, because God's love has been poured into our hearts through the Holy Spirit that has been given to us.
Romans 5:5 (NRSV)

The new year seems to be a hopeful time for most people. It represents an opportunity for a fresh start. All too often, though, the hope with which we begin the year wanes more quickly than we imagined. After the joy and celebration of Christmas, we resume the routines of work, church, family life and community involvement. The same old patterns can fill our time and sap some of the freshness and hope from our year.

This is not to say that hope fades entirely. Faith in God calls us to live lives of hope and to be beacons of hope for others. The hope we find in God is lasting in a way that the hope of a new year can never be. Hope in God grounds us in the eternal awareness of God's abundance, mercy and love. The challenge is to embrace and live out this hope day by day.

In this issue, writers give us glimpses and offer examples of how they find and sustain their hope in God during challenging times and in joyful ones. I pray that these stories will encourage and inspire all of us to find new practices and habits of hope that will keep us rooted in God's love and help us to become beacons of hope for others in the year ahead.

Lindsay L. Gray
Editorial Director, The Upper Room

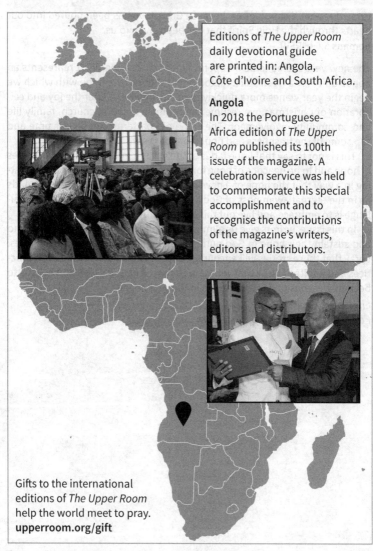

Editions of *The Upper Room* daily devotional guide are printed in: Angola, Côte d'Ivoire and South Africa.

Angola
In 2018 the Portuguese-Africa edition of *The Upper Room* published its 100th issue of the magazine. A celebration service was held to commemorate this special accomplishment and to recognise the contributions of the magazine's writers, editors and distributors.

Gifts to the international editions of *The Upper Room* help the world meet to pray.
upperroom.org/gift

The Editor writes...

The wisteria that spread along the length of the cottage near where I live had surpassed itself. Its huge, mauve, pendant-like flowers cascaded down the wall, causing passing walkers and indeed motorists to slow down and take a long look at one of spring's most beautiful sights. Gusts of perfume filled the air as the flowers swayed gently in the breeze.

All too soon, the magnificent flowering season began to draw to a close for another year as spring turned into summer, and the colours began to fade and die. Yet still, even from the dying flowers there came a lovely scent, perhaps even more powerful than before. It was as if the plant was putting out a last effort for this year, in its continuing cycle of life.

I thought then of Paul's words in 2 Corinthians 2:14–15: 'But thanks be to God, who… uses us to spread the aroma of the knowledge of him everywhere. For we are to God the pleasing aroma of Christ among those who are being saved and those who are perishing' (NIV).

What does it mean to be the 'pleasing aroma' of Christ? Are people drawn to our words and our character as they are drawn to see and smell a perfect flower? Are we doing our best to spread the knowledge of Jesus' saving grace to those who have maybe never experienced or even heard of it? Does our example of Jesus' love provide something of value when we share it with others?

One day, our efforts to live in and for Jesus will draw to a close, at least in this life. What 'aroma' will we leave behind us? We would all like to be remembered with affection by our families or respect from our peers, but what will we leave behind that reminds others of Jesus?

In all our days, we can try to be the 'pleasing aroma of Christ' to each person we meet.

Susan Hibbins
UK Editor

The Bible readings are selected with great care, and we urge you to include the suggested reading in your devotional time.

Time flows away

Read Psalm 90:1–12

Teach us to count our days that we may gain a wise heart.
Psalm 90:12 (NRSV)

In our family we have a tradition of reading Psalm 90 on the night of 31 December, as we pass into the new year. I enjoy this opportunity to reflect on the mystery of the passing of time and of my passing with it, on the transience of human life. I like the sensory image of life fading away and being renewed (vv. 5–6): 'In the morning it flourishes and is renewed; in the evening it fades and withers.' These words invite me to take a personal inventory of my earthly days. A great many are already behind me, with perhaps only a few still to come.

Looking back, I see countless signs of God's grace: the beauties of creation, new discoveries in science, access to the Bible, the joys and warm delights of a large family, good health, music and the arts, sports and, especially, belonging to a lively Christian congregation.

Looking to the future, I also feel a moment of sadness as the shadow of human mortality passes over me and I realise that all earthly life could be over at any time. But a moment later I rejoice, for I am sure that the Lord still has a plan for me beyond this life: eternal life in the light of God's glory.

Prayer: *God of all our years, thank you for giving us blessings every day and opportunities to follow you. Amen*

Thought for the day: God's hand has led me, is leading me and will lead me tomorrow.

Giunio Censi (Lombardy, Italy)

The bigger picture

Read Ephesians 4:25–32

Be kind to one another, tender-hearted, forgiving one another, as God in Christ has forgiven you.
Ephesians 4:32 (NRSV)

Growing up I had a challenging relationship with my father. Though I knew he loved me, he often hurt my feelings by the things he said to me or the way he said them. I grew up thinking all sorts of negative things about myself that simply were not true.

As I grew older, God helped me to see that I was focusing on myself and my own hurt and not seeing the bigger picture. I realised that Dad's words were not always a result of my actions or presence but were more often a reflection of his own childhood trauma, fear and brokenness. One day, he belittled me in front of my daughter. God softened my heart to say, 'Dad, why did you say that?' He said, 'When it's time for your visit to end, I feel hurt – but I shouldn't take it out on you.' I realised then that he simply didn't know what to do with the pain he was feeling.

I wondered how many times I, too, had lashed out at others, or even God, out of fear or pain. I am grateful now that God has freed me from the pain of emotional abuse. Now, when someone speaks to me in an unkind way, I am better able to be tender-hearted and not take it personally. Knowing that God loves and affirms me, I can regard others – and myself – with compassion.

Prayer: *Father God, help us to see the confusion, hurt or anger of others and to offer love where there is insult. Amen*

Thought for the day: Today I will offer God's love in places of pain.

Kristen Lowe (Wisconsin, US)

Showers of blessing

Read Ezekiel 36:24–28

*Blessed are those whose transgressions are forgiven, whose sins
are covered. Blessed is the one whose sin the Lord will never count
against them.*
Romans 4:7–8 (NIV)

On a particularly wet day I put my waterproof trousers and jacket
over my outdoor wear, donned sturdy boots and set off to walk to my
book-club meeting, despite the weather. Because I was well covered
up, I stayed absolutely dry inside while enjoying the mile-long walk in
the heavy rain. There were few other people around, and I was able to
meditate as I walked.

While the rain poured down on me, it made me think of God's forgiveness, washing away my sins, so that I can treasure walking closely
with him on even the stormiest of days.

Jesus' sacrifice on the cross means that our guilt is removed and
replaced with his righteousness, so that we can walk in newness of life.

As I took off my dripping rainwear when I was safely inside, it was
good to reflect that God's love is never removed from his children.

Prayer: *Heavenly Father, we thank you for your love that enfolds us all
and covers our faults. Keep us ever grateful for Jesus' sacrifice for us,
which washes us clean. Amen*

Thought for the day: No matter what I am going through, knowing
Jesus puts joy in my heart and a spring in my step.

Christine Hay (Scotland, United Kingdom)

In the new year

Read Lamentations 3:19–26

[The Lord's compassions] are new every morning; great is [God's] faithfulness.
Lamentations 3:23 (NIV)

As the new year approached, I took some time to look back on this past year. I thanked God for the abundant blessings, favour and grace I had experienced. But I also remembered how many times I had complained to God this past year. Whenever his plans differed from what I wanted, I asked, 'Why, Lord? Do you really love me?' But then, as time passed, I would realise that God's plans for me were always best.

This year, one of my resolutions is to avoid complaining to God, regardless of my circumstances. It is not an easy resolution. I may suffer hardships or disappointment. I may be tempted to complain again and ask, 'Why, Lord?' I am aware of this, but I know that God's strength is always with me. God has blessed me in past years and will continue to bless me. I believe his love and compassion are new every morning.

Even though I cannot know how this year will turn out, I choose to live with faith and hope, trusting that God will do many great things in my life. Thanks be to him for the years past, and thanks be to him for this new year.

Prayer: *Beloved God, thank you for your love and faithfulness. Help us always to cling to you, both during our struggles and through each day of our lives. Amen*

Thought for the day: God's love and faithfulness enable me to live with hope.

Linawati Santoso (East Java, Indonesia)

Giving with love

Read Luke 21:1–4

[Jesus said,] 'All these people gave their gifts out of their wealth; but [this poor widow] out of her poverty put in all she had to live on.'
Luke 21:4 (NIV)

When my husband and our two-and-a-half-year-old great-grandson Carson returned from a walk one morning, Carson handed me what was left of a rose. Apparently, it had already wilted when he found it, and on the way home all but one rather sad-looking petal had fallen off. In spite of that, I valued it just as much as I would a perfect rose fresh from a florist's shop, because it was a gift from a person I love.

That's the way it is when we offer whatever we have to God with all our love. Jesus took notice when the woman in today's reading gave her two small coins to the temple treasury. When we give of our time, talents and money to God, it is precious in his eyes. I'm sure God loves to see us take time to study the Bible and pray, use our talents to help someone or give money to our churches and people in need. What we have to offer may seem less than what others have to give; but instead of comparing our gifts to others', God measures only the love with which we give them.

Prayer: *Dear Father, help us to give with joyful and generous hearts. As Jesus taught us, we pray, 'Father, hallowed be your name, your kingdom come. Give us each day our daily bread. Forgive us our sins, for we also forgive everyone who sins against us. And lead us not into temptation.'* Amen*

Thought for the day: I want to offer God the best of what I have.

Joanne Fleck (Oregon, US)

PRAYER FOCUS: CHILDREN LEARNING TO GIVE
*Luke 11:2–4

Go and glow

Read Matthew 5:13–16

Let your light shine before people, so they can see the good things you do and praise your Father who is in heaven.
Matthew 5:16 (CEB)

When I think about being a light to the world, I remember one of my favourite childhood toys: a glow-in-the-dark, synthetic-rubber super ball. If I carried it in my pocket all day, it was merely a ball that could bounce really high. But if I left it out in the sun, it would provide hours of night-time play with its green glow.

I think my faith journey often resembles that little ball. On days when I am able to focus on God and his presence – through prayer, time reading the Bible, acts of service – I can almost feel a glow from within. And like the ball, the brightness of my shining is dependent on regular contact with a greater source of light.

Jesus has called us to be his light to the world. I believe those who shine are meant to move out into the night. Just as objects that glow are most useful in the dark, so our simple loving presence in a troubled world has great value.

Still, we all face days when we don't feel all that shiny and bright. During those times, it helps me to think about tiny light sources such as a match, a small torch or my childhood super ball. When we try to help others, even our faintest glow can serve as a beacon of God's love.

Prayer: *Dear God, fill us with your light and love. Guide us into opportunities today and every day where we can brighten the lives of others. Amen*

Thought for the day: How can God use me to light the world?

Patrick Klingaman (Maine, US)

Beyond all imagining

Read Philippians 4:4–7

God has prepared things for those who love him that no eye has seen, or ear has heard, or that haven't crossed the mind of any human being.

1 Corinthians 2:9 (CEB)

Throughout my career as a journalist I held important jobs with a good salary to match. However, in 2016 I was dismissed from one of the most prominent television stations in Colombia. That same year, my husband's business ventures began to slow down. We became deeply concerned, so we made some changes. We sold our car and moved into a smaller house. Then, because we had not been able to reduce our credit card debt, we had to leave that house, too. But no estate agency was willing to rent a house to us. The outlook was bleak.

One evening, I began to pray in earnest and delve into the word of God. Today's verse spoke to me. As I read this, I cried and asked God for a miracle. That evening while walking around the neighbourhood, I saw a 'For Rent' sign posted in front of a house nearby. I knocked on the door. The owner greeted me and told me she had been praying that God would send someone to whom she could rent her house. She had to move precisely at the time we had to move out of our own house.

That night as I prayed, I gave thanks to God for possibilities and opportunities that were far beyond what I could have imagined.

Prayer: *God of hope, thank you for hearing our prayers. Strengthen our faith to see your higher purpose for us. Amen*

Thought for the day: My help comes from the Lord (see Psalm 121:2).

Jimena Cortes (Colombia)

Children of God

Read Romans 8:12–17

In Christ Jesus you are all children of God through faith, for all of you who were baptised into Christ have clothed yourselves with Christ.
Galatians 3:26–27 (NIV)

On the first day of each community-college art class I taught, I would ask the students to write a brief answer to the question, 'Who are you?' Later, I was eager to read their responses. One of the answers I've never forgotten was, 'I am a child of God.' This young woman's response left me in awe that she was so grounded in her faith. It also led me to question myself: 'Is my faith so strong that I would have replied in this way?' I probably would have listed my education and work accomplishments. I realised that the growth I should always be most willing to share with others is my deepening relationship with my heavenly Father.

God gives me grace and has been with me all the days of my life. He is there during good times and bad, and he comforted me when my husband died. God loves me unconditionally, answers my prayers and guides me.

Years ago, that student enriched my life by helping me become more aware of my faith. I have learned that I am a child of a merciful God who asks me to encourage my sisters and brothers. God rejoices when I reach out to others, encouraging them to join his family.

Prayer: *Dear Lord, help us live in unity and serve you as we reach out to others and share with them your message of hope and love. Amen*

Thought for the day: My identity rests in God.

Lois E. Wilson (Ohio, US)

The water of life

Read John 4:7–15

Jesus answered, 'Very truly, I tell you, no one can enter the kingdom of God without being born of water and Spirit.'
John 3:5 (NRSV)

I once worked for a building company on new housing developments. Our job was to connect houses to the water system. The work was not always easy, but it was worth the effort. When we turned on the water, a once-quiet house suddenly seemed alive – we knew it was only a matter of time before that house would become a home. It amazed me that the house could be transformed so quickly when we just turned on a valve.

There was a time in my life when I felt a lot like one of those empty houses. Growing up, I didn't have the Lord in my life. When I started going to church and spending time reading the Bible daily, I began to experience the living water of God's presence in my life. Like those houses, when I finally connected to God's word and began living his way, I felt my spirit filled with new life. I know that I won't be empty any more. I have a relationship with God that I once thought I would never have with anyone. Like the empty houses, I have been transformed forever by God's living water.

Prayer: *Heavenly Father, help us to remember that you are the living water. Thank you for transforming our emptiness into abundant life. Amen*

Thought for the day: God's love can always give me life.

Mark A. Carter (Oregon, US)

From fear to hope

Read Ephesians 6:10–17

God hath not given us the spirit of fear; but of power, and of love, and of a sound mind.
2 Timothy 1:7 (KJV)

Depression has afflicted my life in different ways over the years. One constant was fear – the persistent catch in my chest that made it difficult to ever be completely at ease. It felt as if everything had the potential to fill me with fear. Often I would awake in a cold sweat, in the grip of the terror and dread of a panic attack. I would lie trembling in my bed, too terrified to get up and switch on the light.

For me, the greatest revelation in the verse quoted above was that God did not give me a spirit of fear but rather a spirit of a sound mind. One of the counsellors at church advised me to rely on this verse, but, to be honest, I did not believe this would help in any way. Still, the next time the terror came I recited the verse and continued to repeat it – mostly because I did not know what else to do.

It became my nightly declaration. Then, many weeks later, I realised that the fear had lessened. The repetition of this truth from God's word had helped reduce my fear. God's word is powerful enough to enable me to stand firm and be courageous.

Prayer: *Dear God, thank you for your word. Help us to rely on it with the sure knowledge that you will always give us strength. In Jesus' name. Amen*

Thought for the day: With God's word to encourage me, I can stand firm.

Teresa Naidoo (KwaZulu-Natal, South Africa)

Found!

Read Luke 15:1–10

[Jesus said,] 'I tell you, there is rejoicing in the presence of the angels of God over one sinner who repents.'
Luke 15:10 (NIV)

When I was a child, the tropical outdoors of Nigeria where I lived beckoned to me, and I loved to play outside. On the grass, rocks, dirt, mud, cement patio – whatever the setting – I had a toy car that would keep me happily playing for countless hours. Sometimes, other children would join in, each adding to our games.

Now and then, our toys would be lost – sometimes for good. Once, my toy car was washed away in the rainy season, only to reappear in a different area. When I found it, I was delighted. It didn't even matter that by this time it had begun to show signs of rust and discoloration or that the wheels didn't roll well anymore. My toy car, which once was lost, had been found!

Today's passage speaks of other treasured things being lost and then found – a sheep found by a shepherd and a woman's lost coin. For me, it was a beloved toy. All of these situations help us to understand the delight God feels when a lost sinner is found.

Prayer: *Heavenly Father, we acknowledge that we were all once lost. Thank you for loving us enough to send your Son to save us. In his name, we pray. Amen*

Thought for the day: I can rejoice with God and the angels in heaven when a lost one is found.

Ron Wasson (Texas, US)

A remarkable opportunity

Read Matthew 3:1–12

In those days John the Baptist came, preaching in the wilderness of Judea.
Matthew 3:1 (NIV)

In the 1970s, one winter afternoon after college, I hurried to Moscow's State Tretyakov Gallery to study a painting entitled *Appearance of Christ before the People* by Alexander Ivanov. My plan was to sit alone and reflect on the life-size masterpiece, but a young stranger soon joined me on the bench. 'Can you explain it?' he asked.

'The setting is 2,000 years ago,' I began. I went on to point out the Roman soldiers on horses and John the Baptist holding a staff near the Jordan River. I explained that John was calling people to repent because God was sending a Messiah to save them. 'In the distance we see Jesus Christ approaching. Though he never sinned, he will persuade John to baptise him. The story is in the Bible.'

'Have you ever seen a Bible?' the young man asked. I pulled a small Russian Bible from my handbag, opened it to Matthew 3 and, with a silent prayer, watched him read. Filled with wonder, I realised that God offers us opportunities in our daily encounters to meet people who need to hear about Jesus.

Prayer: *Dear God, help us to share your word with people who cross our path every day. Amen*

Thought for the day: Interruptions are often opportunities from God.

M. J. George (Indiana, US)

My right place

Read Romans 12:4–8

Just as the body is one and has many members, and all the members of the body, though many, are one body, so it is with Christ.
1 Corinthians 12:12 (NRSV)

The most beautiful plant in our home is in our bathroom. It is a November cactus, and it amazes us with its beautiful flowering, even in conditions where other flowers fight for their existence, like the short winter days. In the bathroom, it has found its right environment to blossom.

In the same way, it is vital that we as humans find our right environment so that we can blossom. Each of us is original and valuable – just as we are.

The November cactus does not need much light, so it does well in the shade. Similarly, not all Christians require being in the spotlight to make life meaningful. The important thing is that we find our right place, so that in those conditions and with the gifts God has given us, we can bring hope and share in God's kingdom. The potential to blossom exists within each of us so that we can serve among people in our community, in our country and in our world.

Prayer: *Dear God, help us to discover the gifts we have received, and make us willing to use them for you so that our lives can flourish to your glory. Amen*

Thought for the day: Today I will seek the places where I can best use my talents to serve the Lord.

Nils-Åke Nilsson (Sweden)

Lavishly loved

Read Psalm 139:1–6

See what great love the Father has lavished on us, that we should be called children of God!
1 John 3:1 (NIV)

One of my patients has dementia, and her husband of 50 years is doing everything he can to care for her. He washes her soiled clothes, provides her meals and arranges all the doctor's appointments. Several times a day, he patiently explains to her why her brother is in hospital, even though he's already told her many times before.

As I sat there watching them, I was overcome by their genuine love. Theirs is sacrificial and committed – a love that knows every intimate detail and doesn't give up. In that moment, I remembered that Christ's love for each of us runs so much deeper than even the love my patient and her husband have experienced in their marriage. What other love would cause someone to lay down his life for a sinner like me?

Out of great love, God is concerned with every detail of our lives. He knows our thoughts, actions and ways – the words we speak even before we can voice them. God is ever-present and not far away. He has moulded us into who we are. How can we feel anything but loved?

Prayer: *God, who is love, help us to remember that you love us despite our many imperfections. Guide us to love others in that same way. In Jesus' name, we pray. Amen*

Thought for the day: God's love can never be taken from me.

Alisha Ritchie (North Carolina, US)

Watch and pray

Read Matthew 26:36–41

The prayer of a righteous person is powerful and effective.
James 5:16 (NIV)

At the beach one Saturday, I was doing some fishing while watching the sun rise. The brilliant colours that emerged were stunning. This awesome sight caused me to pause to thank God for another day in his beautiful creation – to enjoy the waves, the breeze, the birds and the fish I was expecting to catch. As I finished giving thanks for the many blessings of the morning, a fishing friend arrived and we spent time talking about prayer. He admitted that he found it hard to find time for consistent prayer because of his busy lifestyle. He asked me how I found the time.

I explained that a long time ago I discovered an easy method after reading Jesus' instruction to the disciples to watch and pray. I decided that every time I looked at my watch to see what time it was, the time was right for me to pray. I made it a habit to pray for whatever was on my mind or what was going on at that time. Soon I was praying at least ten times a day. My friend tried it and found that he had more time to pray than he had realised.

Other methods could be to pray during commercial breaks while watching a TV programme or on our morning commute. With some creativity and intention, we can always find time to pray.

Prayer: *Heavenly Father, thank you for the opportunity to share our petitions with you at any time, in any place and for anything. In Jesus' name, we pray. Amen*

Thought for the day: Every day I have unlimited opportunities to pray and give thanks.

Edward Mitchell Jr. (Florida, US)

Isn't it glorious?

Read Revelation 21:1–7

'[God] will wipe every tear from their eyes. There will be no more death' or mourning or crying or pain, for the old order of things has passed away.
Revelation 21:4 (NIV)

I teach creative writing to adults, including many older adults. Recently I learned that one of my students had died after a short, intense illness. It wasn't easy sharing this news with the others, but we took time to remember our friend. My favourite memory is of her breezing into class on a wet, wild, grey winter's day and proclaiming, 'Isn't it glorious!' I thought she was joking at first. 'Oh no,' she said. 'I absolutely love this weather. My dog and I had a wonderful walk on the beach. It makes you feel alive!'

I always appreciated her upbeat outlook, and I knew she had been a strong Christian. I'm certain that her pain is gone and now she is feeling more alive than ever.

Today's reading from Revelation reminds us that our present sufferings are only temporary. God will make us whole once again – more whole than we've ever been. And as we enjoy our life here on earth, we can remember that God's home is now among us. God alongside us and God to look forward to: isn't it glorious?

Prayer: *Heavenly Father, we praise you for our eternal hope and for your presence alongside us. Amen*

Thought for the day: My hope in God is for today and for eternity.

Caroline Greville (Kent, United Kingdom)

On the team

Read 1 Corinthians 12:8–27

You are the body of Christ, and each one of you is a part of it.
1 Corinthians 12:27 (NIV)

As a young boy, I fantasised that my first day on the football team would be the beginning of a major career. However, my father's war injury had prevented him from teaching me how to play football, so my inability to pass accurately or strike at the goal relegated me to the subs' bench. What hurt the most was that the coaches ignored me in order to focus on the more promising team members. The next year we moved to a town with a YMCA. In their sports programmes, everyone got to play, regardless of talent or experience. Friendly coaches worked with me to improve my basic skills. They emphasised self-improvement, goal set-ting and teamwork. The Christlike attitude I witnessed at the YMCA led me to a deeper life of faith.

The church is the body of Christ, and Jesus wants everyone to play on his team. He does not want anyone to be ignored or to be on the bench. In the body of Christ, everyone can find opportunities to grow spiritually through worship, study and service.

Prayer: *Dear Lord, thank you for making us a part of your church. May we help to lead others to a life of faithful service. In Jesus' name. Amen*

Thought for the day: I will encourage someone to become an active part of the body of Christ.

Leland P. Gamson (Arizona, US)

God in the small things

Read 1 Kings 18:41–45

The seventh time [Elijah's] assistant said, 'I see a small cloud the size of a human hand coming up from the sea.'
1 Kings 18:44 (CEB)

One of my nephews called to tell me that he had lost the identity bracelet I gave him for his birthday and wanted to know where I had bought it. I remembered the day I bought it for him. I didn't have a lot of money but just wanted to send him a token of love on his birthday. Even though it was not a big, expensive gift, God had used it to encourage my nephew. From that experience I have learned to look for God in the small things.

That reminds me of our reading today. The prophet Elijah began to pray for relief from a drought that had lasted three-and-a-half years. He sent his assistant to look for a sign that rain was on the way. The servant went back seven times before he saw it: a cloud as small as a human hand. That was all the evidence they needed to know that God was about to move in a big way.

We can look for God in all situations. The problems we have may not go away overnight, but often we can find something to be grateful for. And a grateful heart can change our outlook.

Prayer: *Dear Lord, thank you for the assurance of your love and presence with us. Help us to see you in every situation in our lives. Amen*

Thought for the day: What small sign of God's presence have I seen today?

Tommie Savage (Alabama, US)

In his name

Read John 14:1–14

[Jesus said,] 'You may ask me for anything in my name, and I will do it.'
John 14:14 (NIV)

I was born into a Christian family, but I married a non-believer. After 25 years of marriage, my husband was hospitalised. The doctor said that the infection in his blood would continue to cause him muscular aches and pains and headaches as his body became thinner and weaker.

I decided to encourage my husband to believe in God by telling him that I trust God in every circumstance, whether through times of health or of illness. The doctor did not yet know the cause of this illness, but I knew that my Lord was aware and ready to help. At that time, I gave my husband Bible verses to read so that he could join me in praying for God to be with us.

Over the course of two weeks, we petitioned God in the name of Jesus Christ. As a result, my husband decided to accept Jesus Christ and devote all his life to him. Our two Christian children and I rejoiced that he had joined us in Christ, and together we trusted in God while my husband was being treated in the hospital and eventually was healed.

Prayer: *God of mercy, teach us to believe and trust in you. Help us to be examples of faith in all that we do. In the name of Jesus Christ. Amen*

Thought for the day: Every day I will pray for those who do not know Christ.

Pratoom Pongjai (Phrae, Thailand)

Inner strength

Read Ephesians 3:16–21

I pray that out of his glorious riches he may strengthen you with power through his Spirit in your inner being.
Ephesians 3:16 (NIV)

On my first trip to New York City, I was greatly impressed by the tall skyscrapers that form the Manhattan skyline. However, the exteriors of these structures conceal much more than they reveal. The buildings can reach so high only because of what is inside them. They are fortified inside with steel, concrete and wire mesh. This reinforcement allows the building to rise upwards and remain stable and strong, even when storms come and winds blow. Each structure is a marvel of engineering and construction – on both the outside and the inside.

Our Christian lives resemble these tall buildings more than we realise. Only when we look to God – the ultimate architect and engineer – are we best equipped to weather the storms of life. God is our inner strength when this world throws difficult and demanding situations at us. Prayer, Bible study and worship are to our Christian lives what concrete and steel are to tall buildings. We can remain strong and stable with the assurance that God will always give us the inner strength to meet whatever challenges come our way.

Prayer: *Dear Lord, help us to seek the power of your unfailing strength in our lives. Lead us and guide us safely through the storms of life. Amen*

Thought for the day: Christ is my inner strength.

James Townsend (Mississippi, US)

The blessing of forgetting

Read Psalm 103:8–14

Forgetting what lies behind and straining forward to what lies ahead, I press on towards the goal for the prize of the heavenly call of God in Christ Jesus.
Philippians 3:13–14 (NRSV)

It happened again! I simply could not remember the name of a friend – someone I had known for ages. Her name had totally slipped my mind. When it finally came back to me, I dismissed my forgetfulness as another 'senior moment'.

I began to think about how terrible and sometimes embarrassing it can be to be forgetful. And then I thought of one kind of forgetfulness that I am certainly thankful for – that my sins are removed and forgotten by God. As Jeremiah 31:34 states, 'I will forgive their wrongdoing and never again remember their sins' (CEB). I am forever grateful that God forgets my sins. I began to thank God for forgiving my sins and also for helping me to forget, as I forgive others who have hurt me over the years. Like Paul, I also strive to forget all that lies behind me – including my disappointments and past mistakes. Forgetting these helps me to forgive myself and to look to the future with hope.

I have often heard others state, 'I have forgiven, but I can't forget.' For humans that is very probable. But praise God for not only forgiving but forgetting as well!

Prayer: *Gracious God, thank you for forgiving and forgetting our sins when we confess them to you. In Jesus' name. Amen*

Thought for the day: God forgives and forgets my sins.

Rebecca Seaton (Tennessee, US)

Befriending God

Read Psalm 21:1–7

You bestow on him blessings forever; you make him glad with the joy of your presence.
Psalm 21:6 (NRSV)

Being the last child born in my family, I had no younger brothers or sisters to carry or to play with; all my siblings were a lot older than me. In search of something to care for and to befriend, I picked out a little lamb from my father's flock that became my friend. I carried it around all the time. When it grew into a sheep, I could not carry it any longer; but the closeness remained and it followed me everywhere.

My friendship with that lamb helped me to understand that God longs to have just such a relationship with us. When we allow God to carry us, we begin to grow closer and to know him more deeply. Then as we grow in our faith, we will follow him more closely.

I experienced this some months ago when I made a decision to have a closer relationship with God, and I started spending more time reading the Bible each day. As I kept doing this, my desire to follow and obey God intensified. I experienced joy and fulfilment in God's presence that I had never known before – it changed my life. To this day, I have a desire to stay in God's presence daily because I have tasted the sweetness it brings. We have everything to gain by spending time with God.

Prayer: *Dear Lord, give us a desire to spend time in your presence day by day, as we read your word. Give us the fullness of joy that comes from a relationship with you. In Jesus' name. Amen*

Thought for the day: The time I spend reading the Bible is never wasted.

Enid Adah Nyinomujuni (Dar es Salaam, Tanzania)

Free up space

Read Matthew 11:28–30

[The Lord] lets me rest in grassy meadows; he leads me to restful waters.
Psalm 23:2 (CEB)

During the Sunday morning service I was leading, I asked three people from the congregation to stand at the front. I then asked them to arrange themselves from the busiest to the least busy person. The busiest person had to hold two giant boxes. The next held a stack of books and the last held nothing. I then told them they had to catch a ball that I would throw to them. I threw the ball to each person, and only two out of the three caught it. I explained that the ball represented opportunities from God and that if we are too busy, we won't be able to catch what God is tossing to us.

That afternoon, when I got home after the service, I realised how busy I was myself. Between work, leading the Boy Scouts, worship band, choir, friends and church, my arms were pretty full. We have control over much of the busyness of our lives. When we free up some space, we allow God to give us rest and are able gladly to receive the opportunities that come our way.

Prayer: *God of rest, teach us to lay down our burdens and find rest in you so that we won't miss the opportunities you send us. Amen*

Thought for the day: What can I give up in order to act on the opportunities that God is giving me?

Timothy Sandridge (Virginia, US)

Wrestling with God

Read Genesis 32:22–30

Consider it pure joy… whenever you face trials of many kinds, because you know that the testing of your faith produces perseverance.
James 1:2–3 (NIV)

After Jacob had wrestled with a stranger, this stranger gave him a new name. The man said, 'Your name will no longer be Jacob, but Israel, because you have struggled with God and with humans and have overcome' (Genesis 32:28). Through his struggle, Jacob changed. He was not the same person as before.

Perhaps at one time or another, all believers have felt as if they have been wrestling with God. I feel this way when I'm searching for a new job. For some people, this task may not be particularly stressful; but at times in a job search I have felt as if I were in a tug of war with God and with the people involved. I struggle to deal with one rejection after another, to pray, to send out more CVs and to make more phone calls – in what at times feels like a losing battle to prove myself. All the time I try to be content that my task is to trust the Lord while I search. Like Jacob, after an encounter with God I am not the same person as before.

I have learned that when we are faithful, our wrestling is not in vain. In whatever we are struggling with today, we can find courage – believing that staying in what seems like a fight may result in a blessing because God is at work.

Prayer: *Dear God, remind us that through our suffering we can learn perseverance and wisdom. Amen*

Thought for the day: In the midst of my struggles, God is working to make me mature and complete.

Rosie DiBianca (California, US)

Praise God!

Read Psalm 150:1–6

I will praise you, Lord, among the nations; I will sing the praises of your name.
2 Samuel 22:50 (NIV)

When I was at college, it was my turn to preach at one of our worship services. I was grateful and eager for the opportunity to proclaim God's word. As I was planning the service in the usual way – first a time of praise, followed by the sermon – God helped me realise that praise isn't confined to the opening part of a service. Praise never ends.

In our daily walk of faith, every loving action we undertake, every service we render, is an act of praise to God. So following the time of music and worship, I began my message proclaiming God's love and faithfulness and spoke of my gratitude for the almighty. The students and teachers listening to the message were also praising God because they opened their hearts and set aside time to commune with him.

In all that we do, wherever we are, we can offer praise to God. All we need is a willing spirit and a desire to praise our marvellous creator.

Prayer: *Holy God, you are worthy of all praise. Help us to praise you continuously in all circumstances. Amen*

Thought for the day: Every act of love is an act of praise.

Daniel E. Mejía Fuentes (Francisco Morazán, Honduras)

Challenge and change

Read Philippians 4:10–13

Trust in the Lord with all your heart and lean not on your own understanding; in all your ways submit to him, and he will make your paths straight.
Proverbs 3:5–6 (NIV)

Life's challenges are many and varied. Some are welcome: leaving home to go to university or to travel; a new job; getting married; becoming a parent or grandparent. Others, such as unemployment, financial worries or ill health, are less welcome. All these challenges call us to accept change and adapt to our new situation.

The apostle Paul gives us a masterclass in dealing with change: he went from being a persecutor of Christians to a preacher of the gospel of Christ. He faced floggings, trials, prison and even a shipwreck! He travelled to many different places, welcomed by some and opposed by others. He was a teacher and encourager, but his path as an apostle was not an easy one. Yet in Philippians 4:11 he says that he has learned to be content in any circumstance, and in verse 13: 'I can do all this through him who gives me strength.'

Accepting change can be daunting, but if we find the courage to seek and trust God's guidance, we will find the pathway that he has set before us, and the strength and peace that he brings.

Prayer: *Heavenly Father, when life brings change, help us to remember that you are there to strengthen and to guide us. Amen*

Thought for the day: I can do everything through him who brings me strength.

Mandy Slade (Somerset, United Kingdom)

Sustained by God

Read 1 Peter 5:6–11

Cast thy burden upon the Lord, and he shall sustain thee: he shall never suffer the righteous to be moved.
Psalm 55:22 (KJV)

As I was reading my *Upper Room* devotion one day, I ran across today's quoted verse. Next to it in my Bible, I had written: 'won't remove the burden but "he shall sustain thee"'. I had written that note long before I lost my beloved husband after nearly 48 years in a very happy marriage. But as I read that Bible verse and my note, they seemed to explain how the Lord has been working in my life.

At times I think I just can't go on living without my husband. But every time I feel that way, along comes a visit, or a note, or a call from a friend or family member. Sometimes I am encouraged by a devotional message that seems to be directed specifically to my situation or a verse that becomes a balm to soothe my broken heart. At other times, when I feel led to help someone else during a time of struggle, it reminds me of how blessed I have been. Helping them helps me too.

The burden of losing my husband hasn't disappeared; but clearly the Lord has put a shoulder under my burden, and I know God will sustain me. I shall not be moved!

Prayer: *Dear God, thank you for faithfully sustaining us through all the grief and trials that we face. Amen*

Thought for the day: In the midst of my suffering, God will help me to help others.

Margie Lank (New Hampshire, US)

Sharing our stories

Read Mark 16:9–20

Many of the Samaritans from that town believed in [Jesus] because of the woman's testimony, 'He told me everything I've ever done.'
John 4:39 (NIV)

I recently met a young woman who shared with me what God had done in her life and how she was determined to remain committed in her relationship with him. It was clear to me that she had not planned to share her story; neither was I expecting to hear any testimony from someone on that particular day. She expressed her confidence and trust in God and her desire to faithfully respond to his call.

Her testimony has totally revived and strengthened my Christian faith. After that encounter, my life hasn't been the same. That conversation has convinced me of how important it is for us to share our stories and testimonies whenever we have the chance. So many people out there need our stories and testimonies in order to experience new life in Christ.

Prayer: *Loving God, open our hearts, minds and mouths that we may tell the world about you. We pray as Jesus taught us, saying, 'Our Father which art in heaven, Hallowed be thy name. Thy kingdom come. Thy will be done, as in heaven, so in earth. Give us day by day our daily bread. And forgive us our sins; for we also forgive every one that is indebted to us. And lead us not into temptation; but deliver us from evil.'* Amen*

Thought for the day: How will I share my faith in God today?

Mavula Sabbath Kefas (Baden-Württemberg, Germany)

Fast and slow

Read Matthew 13:31–33

And I pray that you… may have power… to grasp how wide and long and high and deep is the love of Christ, and to know this love that surpasses knowledge – that you may be filled to the measure of all the fullness of God.
Ephesians 3:17–19 (NIV)

Despite years of healthy eating, much to my annoyance I have developed Type 2 diabetes. Luckily, I don't have a 'sweet tooth', so it hasn't made too much difference to my lifestyle – but I do like sugar in my tea and coffee.

The other day I forgot to put any sweetener in my coffee. I went back and added one, and immediately the drink tasted better. It struck me how quickly it permeated through the drink. I also make my own bread – albeit courtesy of the bread maker these days – but I noticed how slowly the yeast works through the dough, in comparison to the sweetener in my coffee.

Perhaps I am like this as a Christian. Some things I am taught, or read in the Bible, are easy to accept and make a part of my life – they quickly become a part of me. Other things that I try to learn are much harder, and they take a long time to permeate and become a part of my life. But God in his wisdom knows what will benefit me today and in the future, as I grow nearer to him.

Prayer: *Dear Lord, help us to keep growing as your word permeates our lives. Amen*

Thought for the day: Fast or slow, we will be filled with the fullness of God.

Hilary Hartley (Sussex, United Kingdom)

Chimes of God's grace

Read 2 Corinthians 12:6–10

[The Lord] said to me, 'My grace is sufficient for you, for power is made perfect in weakness.' So, I will boast all the more gladly of my weaknesses, so that the power of Christ may dwell in me.
2 Corinthians 12:9 (NRSV)

One very hot day, my lawnmower was not working, so I gave up trying to fix it and went into the house to rest. My two young daughters were visiting their grandparents, and I was lonely and grieving my wife's recent death from cancer. While I was walking towards the back door, a gentle breeze blew through the wind chimes. For a brief moment, it was as though I was hearing the first few notes of an old hymn. I felt encouraged that I was not alone, that God's Spirit and grace were with me.

I have often relearned the message of Paul's experience with his 'thorn in the flesh'. We do not know what his thorn was, but we do know that thorns bring pain. Three times Paul asked the Lord for the thorn to be removed, but the reply was: 'My grace is sufficient for you.' I have learned the truth of Paul's statement from my own life experiences. God's grace is always sufficient. When we trust in God's love for us, he brings unending blessings.

In life, sometimes 'thorns' are removed and sometimes they remain. No matter what, through God's love, we can endure the thorns and still rejoice in his amazing grace.

Prayer: *Dear Father, help us to trust you as we experience the struggles of life and come to know that your grace is always sufficient. In Jesus' name. Amen*

Thought for the day: Even in the midst of tragedy and grief, God's grace is sufficient for me.

Stephen T. Johnson (North Carolina, US)

First rainbow

Read Psalm 33:6–9

[God said,] 'Whenever the rainbow appears in the clouds, I will see it and remember the everlasting covenant between God and all living creatures.'
Genesis 9:16 (NIV)

Last summer, my younger grandson and I went for a week's holiday to my country's beautiful Rila mountains. The weather was changing all the time there. In one day, we experienced sun, rain and even hail. After the storm, a beautiful rainbow appeared in the sky. This was the first time my grandson had ever touched hailstones or seen a rainbow. He was so happy!

I am thankful to the Lord for the time I spent with my grandson and for the beautiful elements of nature he saw. He will have good memories to hold on to in the faraway country where he lives and where rain is rare.

Psalm 24:1–2 tells us: 'The earth is the Lord's, and everything in it, the world, and all who live in it; for he founded it on the seas and established it on the waters.' When we are surrounded by nature, it is easy to look around and see the beauty of it. But we can also look beyond that – to its creator.

Prayer: *Dear God, help us to remember that all you have created is a gift of your love. Amen*

Thought for the day: The beauty of creation reminds me of God's love and glory.

Volya Koruderlieva (Varna, Bulgaria)

Road trip

Read Exodus 13:17–22

People plan their path, but the Lord secures their steps.
Proverbs 16:9 (CEB)

Recently, my wife and I set out on a trip to visit one of our daughters at her university. Thirty minutes into the trip the brake indicator light began flashing on the dashboard. We made a quick decision to return home and change cars before dropping the first car at the garage on our way out. It turned out that the brakes were fine; however, there was a larger issue with the car that would have got worse and caused much further damage – possibly even leaving us stranded. I'm not sure why that indicator light came on, but I am glad that it did.

Sometimes God gives us 'warning lights'. They can come in the form of comments from a friend, a conversation with a stranger, or something we hear on the radio or read in the Bible or in a meditation. It's good to know that God is with us and that he is guiding us. And if we heed God's signs, he will lead us on the right path.

Prayer: *God of all our steps, thank you for lighting our path and for your presence in our lives. Amen*

Thought for the day: Whether or not the path makes sense to me, I will follow God.

Brian Foster (North Carolina, US)

Gathering together

Read Ecclesiastes 4:9–12

Where two or three are gathered in my name, I am there among them.
Matthew 18:20 (NRSV)

I remember playing at being in church as a child. Neighbourhood children, school friends, family members, dolls, stuffed animals and occasionally one of our family pets made up the congregation. We took turns in preaching, teaching, serving Communion, singing and taking the offertory. Our services were never very long, but we had a good time.

Recently, on a cold, winter Sunday morning, I remembered those small childhood gatherings when only three other church members in addition to the minister and the organist entered the church for worship. No one else had braved the cold to join us. Choosing not to be discouraged, we worshipped together.

During his teaching on discipleship, Jesus reminded his followers that where two or three gathered together in his name, he was there with them. I did not realise it at the time, but Christ was with us when we played at being in church as children, just as he was with those of us who gathered in his name on that cold Sunday morning.

Prayer: *Lord God, no matter how many come together, may we always worship you in spirit and in truth. Amen*

Thought for the day: No matter how many people I'm with, God meets me in worship.

Patricia Patton (Texas, US)

Heavenly view

Read Psalm 19:1–6

Set your minds on things above, not on earthly things.
Colossians 3:2 (NIV)

The old birch tree that used to grow in front of my bedroom window had a huge crown of branches and leaves that filled my view out of the window. I loved watching it as the seasons changed each year. Recently disease caused my birch tree to die. At first I was sad, because the view of the outside from my window looked so empty and desolate. Then I noticed while lying in my bed that for the first time I was able to see the sky from my window. Now I enjoy the many colours of the sky – white clouds and bright blue by day and stars and moon by night. During my quiet time with God, I have a view of the heavens that fills my heart with joy.

At times, however, our Nordic sky is low and grey, making it difficult to see the sun and the night's stars. Similarly, in our spiritual lives, our mistakes and difficulties can sometimes distract us from fellowship with God, even though his mercy never changes. Rather than focusing on what distracts us, we can decide to focus on our relationship with God.

Prayer: *Dear Lord, give us the wisdom to focus on your constant presence rather than our difficulties. Amen*

Thought for the day: What distracts me from spending time with God?

Maire Simm (Tallinn, Estonia)

In God's time

Read Isaiah 49:8–10

'I know the plans I have for you,' declares the Lord, 'plans to prosper you and not to harm you, plans to give you hope and a future.'
Jeremiah 29:11 (NIV)

During a particularly dark moment, after nearly two years of chronic depression, I decided to take my own life. I could not find a reason to move forwards. I had lost hope and had even moved away from God. As I tried to carry out my plan for suicide, a song of worship from long ago began to run through my head; I knew then I could not follow through with my plan. I returned to my car and found a Bible on the back seat. I prayed and opened it at random, and my eyes fell upon Isaiah 49:8: 'In the time of my favour I will answer you… I will help you.' I began to cry when I realised all God had done for me and that he was at work even in this painful time.

I saw in that moment that I can praise God no matter what I am going through. I may not understand where life is going, or why. But knowing that God loves me, that he hears and answers my cries and restores me, helps me to live with hope. Now I take time to reflect on all the good in my life and look for God's blessings even in the darkness.

Prayer: *Thank you, God, for always being with us and for loving us. Help us to encourage one another and to look for opportunities to share hope with those who suffer. Amen*

Thought for the day: I am of infinite value because God loves me.

H. Matthew Francis (Maine, US)

PRAYER FOCUS: THOSE CONSIDERING SUICIDE

'I've been there'

Read Luke 10:25–37

Praise be to… the Father of compassion… who comforts us in all our troubles, so that we can comfort those in any trouble with the comfort we ourselves receive from God.
2 Corinthians 1:3–4 (NIV)

Just before Christmas, a woman with whom I was falling in love informed me that she was dating someone else. I was crushed. At some point, however, I had the idea of seeking out other people who were also dealing with loss. Within a month, I was able to help a woman whose father had died, another sister in Christ who had lost a son to suicide and also a couple whose eldest daughter was rebelling against God.

I believe that many people miss one of the points in the parable of the good Samaritan. It's likely that the priest and Levite who passed by the wounded traveller didn't fully understand what the man was facing in that moment. But the Samaritan, as part of a despised race, understood – probably from personal experience. The Samaritan truly identified with the wounded man's trials; he was able to say, 'I've been there.'

When we are struggling with difficult situations, Jesus calls us to identify with people who are also suffering, who at that point are more our 'neighbours' than others may be. Then we can comfort them with the comfort that we have received from God. By so doing, we imitate Christ and thereby draw closer to God and closer to those around us.

Prayer: *Dear Father, in our hurt, give us the courage to feel the hurts of others and help us to share your comfort with them. In Jesus' name. Amen*

Thought for the day: God wants me to share the comfort I have received with others.

Rick Nowlin (Pennsylvania, US)

My solitary place

Read Matthew 26:36–44

Very early in the morning, while it was still dark, Jesus got up, left the house and went off to a solitary place, where he prayed.
Mark 1:35 (NIV)

When we push our bodies to work without adequate rest or nutrition, we become ill. The same is true of our spiritual lives. During challenging times we may become pessimistic, indifferent to our calling as believers or filled with worry and fear. But Jesus shows us the way to feed our spirituality, even in challenging times. No matter how busy his days were, Jesus always sought out a solitary place and took time to pray and have fellowship with his Father (see Luke 6:12). When Jesus faced difficulties, he always prepared himself by praying.

I have also found that when I am in a solitary place, I can pray openly before God. I kneel and pray in the corner of my bedroom. While my children and my husband are still asleep, I go to that solitary place to prepare myself for the day through prayer and to cry if I need to. After encountering God, I gain new strength – peace in my heart and mind that I cannot get from anywhere else. Not only is my spirit recharged, but my passion for living and walking with God is resurrected. Joy fills my heart and mind despite any obstacles ahead of me.

Prayer: *Dear Lord, please give us honest and humble hearts so that we may find joy and renewed energy to face the day ahead. Amen*

Thought for the day: Where is my solitary place to meet God?

Linda Chandra (Banten, Indonesia)

Loyal love

Read Psalm 89:1–4

Speak to each other with psalms, hymns, and spiritual songs; sing and make music to the Lord in your hearts.
Ephesians 5:19 (CEB)

One of my earliest memories from church is singing hymns while standing next to my father. As we sang, he would point to the words, which gave me confidence to sing along. Because of those memories, music and singing have been important comforters and companions to me. Whether singing while working in the garden or humming a tune at the office, singing is a way to connect to the creator's amazing gift of life and to express our thanks and devotion for his faithful love.

Just as my earthly father guided me along in the hymnbook and later taught me lessons that shaped me, our creator's everlasting love serves as a guide along life's path. Even in dark times, our singing provides a connection to God. Whether it be songs of joy or songs of lament, when we sing it is our testimony and recognition of God's faithful, loyal love for us.

Prayer: *Dear God, help us to remember that your love is with us forever. May songs of praise be ever on our lips and in our hearts. Amen*

Thought for the day: Which song will help me proclaim God's faithfulness today?

John Horany (Texas, US)

Pioneers of faith

Read Psalm 78:1–7

Lord, you have been our dwelling-place throughout all generations.
Psalm 90:1 (NIV)

While researching county records, I found a memoir by a family of pioneers who settled in the same region where my family lived in the 1800s. I was thrilled to discover that this family and mine together built sod houses, planted crops, raised families and established a house of worship amid the prairie's cold, bitter winters and sweltering hot summers. In fact, it was noted that during one particular crisis my great-great-grandfather reminded this close-knit community that God would work things together for their good, as promised in Romans 8:28. It spoke volumes to me that God was his dwelling place, his refuge.

I feel fortunate that over a century ago, my family was trusting in the God whom I worship and trust. I have a legacy of faith, an inheritance of belief – carried down through generations.

The words of Psalm 90 resonate now more than ever. As parents, grandparents or friends, we all have an opportunity to influence the generations that follow. Let us resolve, along with the psalmist, to 'tell the next generation the praiseworthy deeds of the Lord, his power, and the wonders he has done' (Psalm 78:4).

Prayer: *Dear God, help our lives and words to reflect our trust in your amazing power, love and strength. Amen*

Thought for the day: How am I passing on a legacy of faith to those who come after me?

Beverly Taylor (Arizona, US)

Faith like a fire

Read 1 John 4:7–12

If we walk in the light, as [God] is in the light, we have fellowship with one another.
1 John 1:7 (NIV)

Even though the memory is over 50 years old, I can always recall one particular youth meeting. While I do not remember everything – what songs we sang or who was there – I do remember the surroundings and what happened on a certain evening.

A group of us were sitting on a rock that stretched out into the water in the Misterhult archipelago. It was dusk on a cool summer night at the end of an intense day. A campfire was burning under a criss-cross of logs. Without saying anything, one of the leaders removed a log from the fire. After a while, we could see that the log lost its flame while the others still in the fire burned to their fullest. A moment later, someone said, 'We need each other so we can burn bright.' When the log was returned to the campfire, it quickly took the flame again.

This was the message of the preaching that summer – perhaps the most important message of my entire youth. Our faith is like a fire; it burns brightly when stoked with love and community with God and others. God has given us community with one another so that we may give our attention, love and energy to those whose lives intersect with ours.

Prayer: *Dear God, help our love to burn brightly for one another. Amen*

Thought for the day: My faith is brighter when I am in community with God and others.

Tomas Boström (Gotland, Sweden)

Don't you care?

Read Mark 4:35–41

The disciples woke [Jesus] and said to him, 'Teacher, don't you care if we drown?'
Mark 4:38 (NIV)

At first, when Jesus and his disciples were at sea during a terrible storm, Jesus was sound asleep. The waves were threatening all of their lives. 'Teacher, don't you care if we drown?' Those words cut. I'd heard this passage in Mark before, but that day it expressed exactly the doubts I was having about Jesus' caring for me. In the passage, the fearful disciples had snapped. I felt as if I too were snapping. Work, family concerns and financial storms had me feeling battered and ignored. I was losing hope that Jesus could handle my circumstances.

Although the disciples had been full of fear, the storm did not disturb Jesus. Once awake, Jesus called the storm into calm submission. The disciples became even more afraid because Jesus had power over the storm. In that moment he had revealed himself to be the almighty to whom all of creation submits. While he may have been in the storm, he was not subject to it.

I had been feeling as if Jesus were asleep. This story compelled me to confront Jesus with my doubts. Storms don't rattle him. While we are afraid and swamped, he is calm and invites us into his care. He calls us to take courage in knowing that everything submits to him at his command.

Prayer: *Dear Jesus, help us in our storms to stop and see your almighty power. We know that you will deliver us as we trust in you. Amen*

Thought for the day: Jesus invites me into his rest and care.

Randi Perez Helm (Michigan, US)

PRAYER FOCUS: TO FIND PEACE AND REST IN JESUS

The good shepherd

Read Psalm 23:1–6

[The Lord] tends his flock like a shepherd: he gathers the lambs in his arms and carries them close to his heart; he gently leads those that have young.
Isaiah 40:11 (NIV)

While chatting with my cousin I recalled a visit to his farm in Tulbagh, South Africa. Sensing a lamb was in distress, my uncle had invited me to go with him into the fields. Dusk was falling as we headed in the direction of a faint sound. We found a lamb that had fallen into a ditch and was trapped. We were both awed by the prompting that led to the rescue of one lamb.

That memory reinforces my faith in the love of the good shepherd, and I reflect on how God has been with me on my 30-year journey with multiple sclerosis. At a very low point in my life, during a healing service, hands were laid on my head and prayers were offered. Then I heard these softly spoken words: 'God has a special name for you. He calls you his little lamb, and he will pick you up and carry you.'

God knows each of us by name, and Jesus' words from the gospel of John reveal that truth: 'I am the good shepherd; I know my sheep and my sheep know me' (John 10:14).

Prayer: *Loving shepherd, we give you thanks and praise for rescuing and protecting us. Help us to listen for your voice and follow you. Amen*

Thought for the day: The good shepherd knows me by name.

Clare Drew (Gauteng, South Africa)

A rich heritage

Read Joshua 4:1–9

I will remember the deeds of the Lord; yes, I will remember your miracles of long ago.
Psalm 77:11 (NIV)

Ever since he was young, my son has been a curious child. He regularly asks questions of his mother and me and other family members. He wants to know about various family rituals and why we observe certain traditions. We enjoy answering his questions because it gives us the opportunity to share our experiences and history as well as key events that have shaped our lives. Discussing and sharing this information with him often brings us closer to one another and helps him establish his identity within the family.

In the same way, we can take an interest in our church rituals and traditions. Understanding the history of the church, certain events that have shaped it and the story behind rituals and traditions can help us understand the values of our church and the rich heritage that surrounds the community of believers. Sometimes we may even find traditions that transcend denominational boundaries and connect us to the universal church of Christ, bringing us together as one big family, sharing a common Saviour and God.

Prayer: *Our Father in heaven, thank you for sending us your Son, Jesus Christ, to connect us with you. May our traditions and rituals continually remind us of your great love and provide hope for our lives. Amen*

Thought for the day: The traditions of my faith give me vision for the future.

Daniel C. M. Tan (Kuala Lumpur, Malaysia)

Patience

Read Psalm 37:3–6

We know that in all things God works for the good of those who love him, who have been called according to his purpose.
Romans 8:28 (NIV)

I was at the peak of my dance career – training at a dance studio and winning competitions. Then, during class one day, I felt my back twinge. I tried my best to ignore it, but my day ended in hospital. After multiple X-rays, the doctor told my parents and me that I had to choose between surgery or stopping my dancing. I agreed to stop. It was the most difficult decision I had made up to that point in my life.

Somehow, I still felt peaceful about it. The months that followed were full of trials, emotionally and physically. As I sought other pastimes, other passions to replace dance, I found a new love for my relationship with Christ. This was the most fulfilling result that could have happened. I realised that the joy that filled me was not from my ability to dance but from God. I never could have imagined that the Lord would take such a painful loss and turn it into so many blessings.

Every day, I still see blessings that might never have happened if I had chosen differently all those years ago. Of course I miss dancing, but ultimately the passion that I was able to give my relationship with God has been rewarding beyond measure.

Prayer: *Dear God, thank you for everything that you have given us. Help us to wait patiently for what you have in store for us. Amen*

Thought for the day: My relationship with God gives me a fulfilling life.

Rylee Goetzinger (Oklahoma, US)

Choosing mercy

Read Colossians 3:12–17

What does the Lord require of you? To act justly and to love mercy and to walk humbly with your God.
Micah 6:8 (NIV)

I think often about the meaning of Micah 6:8. I love justice, but if justice were up to me, few people would get a second chance. When people are excused from a court hearing because of their declining health, I want them to go to the hearing anyway – if they have made someone suffer then I want them to suffer the consequences. In those moments, I realise that my love of justice is more like a love of retribution. But when I long to see someone punished, am I loving mercy as God calls me to do? When we love mercy, we can rest secure in knowing that God is the perfect judge who will make things right.

As Christians, we can show God's love and grace to the world by being in the business of second chances. Loving mercy, even when it's painfully difficult to do so, is an opportunity to show someone else God's love for us.

Prayer: *Dear God, we thank you that you are a God who gives second chances. We pray that you will strengthen us to do the same for others. Amen*

Thought for the day: I reflect God's love when I show mercy.

Melissa Ramoo (New South Wales, Australia)

'I'm here'

Read Deuteronomy 31:1–8

The Lord your God goes with you; he will never leave you nor forsake you.
Deuteronomy 31:6 (NIV)

On our trips to the beach, my wife, daughter and I like to watch the sunset. One evening while our daughter, Victoria, was sitting on the sand, my wife and I sat on a bench several yards behind her. She was unaware that we had moved some distance away from her. We sat in silence as the red glow of the sun disappeared.

As it became dark, my daughter realised that we were not near her. She called out for us with fear in her voice. When we spoke to her from our bench, she replied, 'I thought you'd left me!' My wife answered, 'We're here; we'd never leave you!'

That conversation reminded me of how often in life we end up in the darkness, thinking we are alone and feeling afraid. When we call out for God's help, it is comforting to know that he will always reply, 'I'm here; I'll never leave you!'

Prayer: *Eternal God, thank you for your faithfulness to us. Strengthen our resolve never to wander away from you. Amen*

Thought for the day: God continually says to me, 'I'm here.'

Jeff Wansley (Georgia, US)

God's reassurance

Read Psalm 33:1–5

The word of the Lord is right and true; he is faithful in all he does.
Psalm 33:4 (NIV)

For most of his life, my 85-year-old husband had been an accomplished musician. He had played the organ, piano, trombone and tuba. But for his last few years he could play none of these. A blood clot on his brain, together with a stroke and a heart attack, had robbed him of these abilities. When Henry died, I mourned the loss of my faithful husband of nearly 64 years, but I also sighed with relief that he no longer struggled to breathe.

About two months after his death, I dreamed that he was booked to play a solo in a concert. Backstage, he kept saying, 'I don't think I can do it.' But when the time came, he stepped onstage and played the most beautiful music he had ever played.

I woke up feeling my grief turned to joy. I remembered that in the Bible God often spoke through dreams, from Abimelek (Genesis 20:3) to the apostle Paul (Acts 18:9–10). In my dream, I felt God was reassuring me that Henry no longer has any physical restraints. In heaven, he is hearing the most magnificent music he has ever heard. And he's helping to provide it in joyful praise to God.

Prayer: *Author of our dreams, may we know the comfort and joy that comes with praising you. Amen*

Thought for the day: In heaven, all my earthly sorrows will be gone.

Virginia Horst Loewen (Pennsylvania, US)

Perseverance in faith

Read Luke 2:25–35

[Simeon] was righteous and devout, looking forward to the consolation of Israel, and the Holy Spirit rested on him.
Luke 2:25 (NRSV)

I find I often lack perseverance and patience in my faith, but I am inspired by the example of my grandparents. They lived through the terror of a Communist regime, but they were not broken by the disappointments of the world. My grandparents prepared to wait a long time and kept their faith strong. They were constant in their expectation and didn't let their love for God cool. With unwavering hope, they waited for his timing.

My grandparents persevered in waiting for God because they loved him. Although they were let down by people, God never let them down. Like Simeon, who faithfully waited for the Messiah's coming, my grandparents remained resolute.

We can teach our children and grandchildren the virtue of perseverance. I pray that we may be examples of perseverance for the next generation so that they can learn what it means to wait for the coming of Christ quietly and full of joy.

Prayer: *Dear Lord, help us to await your coming with perseverance and strong faith. Amen*

Thought for the day: Who has inspired me to persevere in faith?

Daniel Topalski (Varna, Bulgaria)

Answered prayer

Read 2 Corinthians 9:8–15

[The Lord's] divine power has given us everything we need for a godly life through our knowledge of him who called us by his own glory and goodness.
2 Peter 1:3 (NIV)

As I dropped off my daughter at the nursery before Bible study, I chatted with an acquaintance about having to find childcare so I could attend the group's upcoming special lunch. She replied that a friend of hers also needed childcare for a different event. I offered my phone number for her friend, saying that I could probably help. My acquaintance grabbed my hand. 'She has been praying to find a way to attend the event,' she said, 'and maybe you are her answer.'

At the Bible study, I mentioned casually that my husband was on an extended job a long way from home. A woman responded that she knew someone whose husband was in the same situation and travelling to the same location. After giving her my phone number, I received an emotional call from the woman, who said, 'I have been praying that my husband would find a Christian friend in that city.' I was so excited to think that our husbands would be able to encourage each other in a faraway place.

Usually I'm focused on the way God might answer my prayers. Now I understand that I can be God's answer to help or encourage someone else.

Prayer: *Dear God, help us to be sensitive to the needs of others so that we can serve as your answers to the prayers of those around us. Amen*

Thought for the day: I will be ready and alert so that I can act when God needs me.

Susan H. Aaron (Florida, US)

The right question

Read 1 Corinthians 3:6–11

[The Lord declares, 'My word] shall not return to me empty, but it shall accomplish that which I purpose, and succeed in the thing for which I sent it.'
Isaiah 55:11 (NRSV)

While returning home from a night out, my wife noticed a large sign on the verge near a slip road. It read, 'Jesus is the only way to heaven. Where are you going?' My wife asked if I thought such signs were effective. My immediate thought was that they aren't effective. Yet, even as this negative thought came to mind, I realised that we were asking the wrong question. I felt the Spirit asking me, 'When was the last time you shared your faith?' I needed to begin by questioning myself.

Our Lord's final direction to his disciples was, 'Go!' Jesus wants us to participate in the process of making disciples. Instead of criticising someone else's efforts, I should be focused on making efforts of my own.

Each of us is called to share our faith in unique ways. Regardless of our method, Jesus is more than capable of turning our efforts into glorious results. We can trust that Christ's power is at work in the activities of his people. The right question focuses on action and the results are up to God. We need only to be willing.

Prayer: *Dear Lord, please guide us to participate in making disciples for you. Show us the people you have placed in our lives with whom we can share your love. Amen*

Thought for the day: How will I get involved in spreading the gospel?

Stephen Johnson (California, US)

God, the quilter

Read Nehemiah 9:10–17

The one who started a good work in you will stay with you to complete the job by the day of Christ Jesus.
Philippians 1:6 (CEB)

As a quilter for the last 30 years, I have started many projects. Most I have finished, but some that I started with great gusto and magnificent intentions now sit in my sewing corner – untouched and gathering dust. Either I lost interest, they became too difficult to finish or some other project became more important. The once-cherished projects were set aside, forgotten.

Thankfully, God, the quilter of our lives, never responds in this way. Unlike us, our creator 'who started a good work' in us will 'complete the job'. No matter how uninteresting we think we are, how difficult we become or what other projects we think may be more important, God will not leave us in a corner to gather dust. Instead, with great and gracious care, he will keep stitching our lives into a dazzling completed work.

Prayer: *Dear Father, thank you for not setting us aside. Help us to trust that you will finish what you have started as we pray, 'Our Father which art in heaven, Hallowed be thy name. Thy kingdom come, Thy will be done in earth, as it is in heaven. Give us this day our daily bread. And forgive us our debts, as we forgive our debtors. And lead us not into temptation, but deliver us from evil: For thine is the kingdom, and the power, and the glory, forever. Amen'**

Thought for the day: God stitches my life into a heavenly creation.

Jennifer Lanane (North Carolina, US)

PRAYER FOCUS: THOSE WHO PROCRASTINATE
*Matthew 6:9–13 (KJV)

In God's loving arms

Read Psalm 103:1–8

You teach me the way of life. In your presence is total celebration.
Beautiful things are always in your right hand.
Psalm 16:11 (CEB)

In my yoga class we practise a self-hug technique: crossed arms placed on the chest, hands on the shoulders to 'shelter' the heart. One Saturday morning I started with that posture and had a moment of silent prayer. I felt close to Jesus in that moment of calm.

A few hours later, my husband suffered a stroke. I had the presence of mind to get the medical attention he needed quickly. An hour later he underwent an angioplasty procedure. God's grace, along with medical technology, began working to save his life.

Sitting in the waiting room of the hospital, I repeated my morning yoga exercise: self-hug, moment of prayer, close embrace with God. Half an hour before the end of the procedure, I felt that my husband was out of danger. During that moment of prayer and meditation I received a great sense of relief and a deep peace. God's love was far superior to my fear and pain.

That experience was so strong that ever since then, after my devotional time, I take a few moments to remain in that warm embrace – thanking God and holding his love in my heart.

Prayer: *Merciful God, thank you for your infinite love that moves us deeply and shelters us during our most difficult times. In the name of Jesus, we pray. Amen*

Thought for the day: Holding God's love in my heart can bring peace to my day.

Haydée Meloni (Buenos Aires, Argentina)

Created for special purposes

Read 2 Timothy 2:20–21

But we have this treasure in jars of clay to show us that this all-surpassing power is from God and not from us.

2 Corinthians 4:7 (NIV)

I often buy items from our local hospice charity shop, to support the work that they do, and one day I bought a beautiful pottery goblet decorated with a design of oak leaves. For some years it sat on a shelf in our conservatory and although I admired it, it did not fulfil its purpose and remained empty.

Recently I attended an artists' and writers' retreat near where I live. There was much talk about trees at the retreat: we visited an exhibition of tree painting; a lady made a tree sculpture; and I wrote a poem after reading about the strength of tree roots that are fused together. The chaplain also referred to Jesus as a great oak. On the final morning we had an informal Communion service, and it struck me that this would have been the perfect time to use the oak-leaved goblet as a chalice. Later I gave it to the chaplain as a gift, believing that she could use it more than I ever would.

Two months later I attended some days at the next retreat and again attended Communion. I was humbled to see the goblet filled with wine, representing the blood of Christ, being passed from one person to another. Later, I wondered if, like the goblet, I had been an empty vessel. I asked God to fill me, that I might find my purpose in serving him.

Prayer: *Lord, give us courage, and help us to seek and fulfil the purposes you have for us. Amen*

Thought for the day: Today I will seek to serve God in all that I do.

Faith Ford (Herefordshire, United Kingdom)

Confidence for the future

Read Matthew 6:25–34

Do not worry about tomorrow, for tomorrow will worry about itself. Each day has enough trouble of its own.

Matthew 6:34 (NIV)

As I sit in my chair for my morning devotions and look out of my upstairs window, the woods at the back of my house seem dark and forbidding. The leafless trees form ghostly, black silhouettes, much like my thoughts concerning what lies ahead as the years creep by. Will my health fail? Will I be able to meet financial responsibilities? Ageing can be scary. But as I continue my daily appointment with God, I see the first tint of morning sun pierce the horizon. In moments the sky is awash with a pink glow, illuminating the world with glorious new beauty. As I gaze at God's handiwork, I remember that he cares for even the tiniest of creatures, and peace slowly fills my heart.

In Matthew 6:25 Jesus tells us not to worry. Jesus knows the ill effects of worry. It can consume our thoughts, steal our productivity and negatively affect our health. But most importantly, it reduces our ability to trust God. Jesus continues by telling us to seek first God's kingdom by turning to God for help. While planning for tomorrow is time well spent, worrying about what the future holds is just wasted time. We may not know what the future holds, but we can trust the one who holds our hands and walks with us through every dark valley.

Prayer: *Dear Lord, help us to trust you and not to be fearful of what the future may hold, for you have promised never to leave us. Amen*

Thought for the day: God will supply all my needs (see Philippians 4:19).

Jeannine Brenner (Pennsylvania, US)

Service and shoelaces

Read Luke 22:24–30

The one who is greatest among you will be your servant. All who lift themselves up will be brought low. But all who make themselves low will be lifted up.
Matthew 23:11–12 (CEB)

As I returned to my hotel room soaked from the rain, I passed two members of the cleaning staff in the corridor. One of them stopped me and pointed at my untied shoelace. I thanked her but didn't stop to tie it. After all, I was only a short distance from my room. But she stopped me and bent down to tie my shoe.

Although the conference I was attending featured a wonderful speaker and great music, the most powerful lesson I learned that weekend came from this moment of servanthood. Jesus tried to explain to his disciples that God's kingdom was about showing love through seeing and meeting the needs of others. This woman saw a need – which meant that she was paying attention to someone besides herself. Then she unhesitatingly and unselfishly acted to meet it, even though I was a complete stranger. That simple moment in a hotel corridor has motivated me to be more observant, more humble and more willing to meet the needs of those around me.

Prayer: *Dear Lord, help us to see and respond to the needs of others and to fully appreciate the kindnesses shown to us by friends, family or even strangers. Amen*

Thought for the day: If I want to show God's love, I will first be a servant.

John I. Carney (Tennessee, US)

'I still love you'

Read Titus 3:1–7

This is love: not that we loved God, but that he loved us and sent his Son as an atoning sacrifice for our sins.
1 John 4:10 (NIV)

'I don't love you anymore, Gran!' My four-year-old grandson Tim was angrily folding his arms and glaring at me after I'd scolded him for something.

'Oh, but I still love you,' I replied, 'and always will.' Still mad, Tim turned and walked away. But within seconds he was back with a big smile, saying that he was sorry. Of course, I would always love him. He may go astray at times, but we always pray for our children and grandchildren, and never let them out of our hearts. We never stop loving them.

Through Christ Jesus, I am God's child. He loves me and calls me, even when, in my desperate need, I am very far from returning that love. He shows love for me in many ways, including necessary discipline, and is always there for me – even when I don't deserve it.

Titus 3:5 assures me that in mercy God has taken the first steps, and that the Holy Spirit renews our hearts so that we can have the hope of eternal life.

Prayer: *Father God, today help us to rest in your unending love, surrender to your loving discipline and show kindness to all. Amen*

Thought for the day: God loves me more than I can imagine.

Marion Turnbull (Merseyside, United Kingdom)

Rubbish to treasure

Read Psalm 34:17–22
The Lord is close to the broken-hearted and saves those who are crushed in spirit.
Psalm 34:18 (NIV)

Along the coast near my home, craftspeople were selling jewellery made from sea glass, which begins as bottles or glass left on the beach as rubbish. Over time, they are broken into pieces and tumbled by the ocean until sharp edges and shiny surfaces become softened, frosted gems that are then reclaimed. Each piece of the glass is one of a kind, just like each person uniquely created by God.

After talking to an artist about sea glass, I realised that if broken pieces of glass can be transformed into prized treasures, God can do even more for any of us who feel broken, lost or crushed in spirit. No matter how broken we might be, God sees the good in each of us. When we are willing, he can soften sharp edges and sand away our flaws so that we become works of art, shining forth the beauty that God has created in us.

If a discarded piece of rubbish from the sea can be transformed into something of value, think how much more value God places on rescuing each of us – his children!

Prayer: *Dear God, through the power of your presence, transform us to new life now and forever. Amen*

Thought for the day: God can transform my brokenness into something beautiful.

Robert K. Abel (Maryland, US)

Without fail

Read 1 John 5:13–15

This is the confidence we have in approaching God: that if we ask anything according to his will, he hears us.
1 John 5:14 (NIV)

When I was a young girl I loved to visit my grandmother, who lived about 200 miles away. She was a very busy woman – cooking, washing, ironing, gardening and sewing. Every time we visited, she had treats for us to eat, toys for us to play with and games to keep us entertained on rainy days. Each afternoon she devoted time to reading her Bible and then listening to The Gospel Hour on the radio while doing some mending or shelling peas.

One special thing about my grandmother was that she found time, without fail, to listen to others – even to us children. When I'd come to her with a thought or question, she would stop what she was doing and give me her full attention. I can see her face now, smiling and welcoming me.

Years later, when I was having some problems and trying to pray, I kept wondering if God had time to listen to all my seemingly childish thoughts and prayers. Then, the verses above from 1 John reminded me that my grandmother was reflecting the love of God – who is also very busy and yet always welcomes us.

Prayer: *Caring God, we know that when we reveal our thoughts and desires, you are there to listen to, care for and respond to us. Help us always to make time for you. Amen*

Thought for the day: I always have God's full attention.

Linda Birchall (Georgia, US)

God is merciful

Read Proverbs 3:1–10

Heal me, Lord, and I will be healed; save me and I shall be saved.
Jeremiah 17:14 (NIV)

In the winter of 2016, the doctor gave the results to my wife and me: the lesions in my bones indicated multiple myeloma. Yet, no fear came over me. Instead, I was filled with the certainty that I was in God's hands and that he had a plan. For the 40 years of my Christian life, I had lived by these words from the Bible: 'Trust in the Lord with all your heart and lean not on your own understanding; in all your ways submit to him, and he will make your paths straight' (Proverbs 3:5–6). This was the time I would need those verses the most.

After two stem-cell transplants in six months, I was in remission and facing eight months of chemotherapy. Through this battle, God has done amazing things – including reaching people around the world online through two blogs which I update daily, and a thousand poems and songs. My body is strong and getting stronger. God has been very merciful to me.

When facing trials that we do not understand, we can lean on a God who does understand, and whom we can trust in everything that comes our way. We can acknowledge his power and strength through the good things and the bad. Our merciful God can walk with us through anything.

Prayer: *Dear God, help us always to see your mercy that surrounds us each day. When we are afraid, help us to lean on you and trust you to do your work in us. Amen*

Thought for the day: God has been merciful to me.

Peter T. Gardner (Iowa, US)

Always grateful

Read 1 Thessalonians 5:12–18

Give thanks in all circumstances; for this is God's will for you in Christ Jesus.
1 Thessalonians 5:18 (NIV)

One day during our fellowship meeting, our leader spoke about gratitude. After that, he challenged us not to complain about anything for 30 days and to find at least one thing that we could be grateful for each day and write it down.

The leader said, 'Gratitude is a life-changing attitude. When we open our eyes to God's blessings every day, we will find many things for which we can be grateful.' When I thought about my blessings, I found many things that I could be grateful for – the food I eat every day, my healthy body, my happy family, the birds that sing each morning, answered prayers, God's protection and much more.

As we read in the passage quoted above, God wants us to be grateful in all things. Being grateful is a choice. Choosing to be grateful in every situation can keep our hearts filled with joy even during difficult times. Having a grateful heart opens us up to God's blessings in our lives.

Prayer: *Dear God, thank you for your abundant blessings. Help us to give thanks for your grace and goodness in our lives. Amen*

Thought for the day: Gratitude in all things can bring me abundant joy.

Meliana Santoso (East Java, Indonesia)

Casting our nets

Anyone who knows me can attest to the fact that I am set in my ways. While we are all creatures of habit to some extent, I am more routine-oriented than many. When I stop to think about all the things I do over and over each day – at the same time each day – I am a little shocked and confounded. I do not like to deviate from my routine, and even a minor disruption can leave me a little disoriented on some days and decidedly irritable on others.

Routines can be good, but sometimes they can become ruts that prevent me from living in the fullness of life that God wants for me. A rut includes anything from a bad habit to neglect. Speaking from my own experience, a routine becomes a rut when I can imagine no other possible way of doing something – no other way to start or end my day, no other way to respond to a specific situation in my life, no other way to cope with some challenge or difficulty.

As I think about the ruts that I would like to escape from, my mind goes to the story of Peter, Thomas, Nathanael, James, John and two other disciples fishing on the Sea of Galilee in John 21. Scripture says, 'They went out and got into the boat, but that night they caught nothing' (v. 3, NIV). Standing on the shore, Jesus asks them whether they've caught anything. They say no. Jesus then tells them to cast their net on the right side of the boat, and 'when they did, they were unable to haul the net in because of the large number of fish' (v. 6). I can only wonder what the disciples made of this experience and what they learned from it. I would like to think that the next time they found themselves in a similar predicament – doing the same thing over and over without getting any results – they thought back to that night on the Sea of Galilee, when one small change made a dramatic difference.

Breaking away from old habits and worn-out routines can be extremely difficult, scary and anxiety-filled. It often involves letting go of something that we fear we cannot survive without; yet at the end of the day if we remain in our ruts, we turn up empty-handed just like the disciples.

I have decided that this year when I find myself in a rut, I will imagine Jesus standing on the shore, inviting me to cast my net on the other side of the boat. My promise to myself is that I will then accept Jesus' invitation to try something different. Who knows what good might come from it?

What better time than the beginning of the year to start a new, life-giving routine or break away from a habit that is holding us back? What better time to let go of the old so that we can welcome all the new opportunities God wants to send our way? There's no better time than now to cast our nets on the other side of the boat.

Several meditations in this issue address letting go of what holds us back and welcoming the opportunities God wants to send our way. You may want to read again the meditations for 2, 4, 7, 9 and 15 January; 1, 13, 18, 23 and 29 February; 6, 11 and 19 March; and 4 and 11 April before responding to the reflection questions below.

QUESTIONS FOR REFLECTION

1 What old habit or routine would you like to break away from in the coming year? What new one would you like to adopt?

2 Would you describe yourself as a routine-oriented person or not? In what ways can routines and habits be helpful? In what ways can they be unhelpful?

3 When in your life have you 'cast your net on the other side'? What happened? What did this experience teach you?

Andrew Garland Breeden
Acquisitions Editor

Starting the day with God

Read Psalm 5:1–12

In the morning, Lord, you hear my voice; in the morning I lay my requests before you and wait expectantly.
Psalm 5:3 (NIV)

I begin my days by greeting family members. Then, as I come in contact with other people, I greet them. One day I wondered, 'What would happen in my relationships with those I care about if I didn't acknowledge them?' That made me realise that when I first wake up, God is there waiting for me. He deserves to be acknowledged, but what if I don't acknowledge him?

I need God in my life every day, so I decided that when I first wake up and am still lying in bed, I would greet him. Often I thank him for a good night's sleep, and sometimes I complain a little if it was not a good night. Each day, I acknowledge that God is first on my mind. Then I get up.

God deserves our attention, and I have discovered that when he is the first thought of my day, he becomes more important in my daily journey. All through the day, I remind myself that God is with me. When I seek him out first, then the rest of my day is transformed.

Prayer: *Dear Father, remind us to seek you every day. Amen*

Thought for the day: Acknowledging God is my first offering of love each day.

Dean T. Skoglund (Minnesota, US)

How to pray

Read Matthew 21:12–16

[Jesus] said: 'Truly I tell you, unless you change and become like little children, you will never enter the kingdom of heaven. Therefore, whoever takes the lowly position of this child is the greatest in the kingdom of heaven.'
Matthew 18:3–4 (NIV)

One day when my son was praying, I was correcting him and providing him with sentences that I felt should be included in a prayer. Afterwards, my husband told me that we should let him pray in his own words, so the next time I let him say whatever came from his heart. He prayed for various things, and in the end he said, 'Jesus, I am happy with you. Amen.' We were amazed. What a simple way to express gratitude to Jesus!

As we grow up, we tend to focus too much on praying the 'right' way – to speak our prayers so that they will sound correct to those who may hear them. But God sees our hearts, not the complexity of our sentences.

I could never have thought of expressing my love for God in the way that my son demonstrated for me. That day I realised that, yes, we are indeed God's children and he is our Father. We can always talk to God from that perspective. Children have much to teach us about the kingdom of God. Even now I continue to learn how to pray from my son.

Prayer: *Jesus, I am happy with you. Amen*

Thought for the day: Today I will approach God with childlike faith.

Deepika Emmanuel Sagar (Rajasthan, India)

PRAYER FOCUS: CHILDREN LEARNING TO PRAY

Weary with regret

Read Psalm 51:1–17

O Lord, open my lips, and my mouth will declare your praise.
Psalm 51:15 (NRSV)

'I'll never be able to forgive myself.' Just typing these words stirs up so many emotions in me. The years of regret dragged me down; I wore them like chains. Sexual immorality and destructive choices had contributed to my already-low self-esteem. It has taken years, but the story of King David has helped me to accept God's forgiveness and see myself in a positive light.

When the prophet Nathan confronted King David about his affair with Bathsheba, David sought and received God's forgiveness. But if he hadn't accepted God's mercy, that sinful period could have defined the rest of his life. How different would David's story have been if he had chosen to live in self-condemnation? Would we know him as a man after God's own heart? Probably not.

When we choose to hang on to our shame, others see us as guilt-ridden souls rather than people after God's own heart. If we want them to see the relationship we have with God, we can pray King David's prayer after Nathan confronted him: 'O Lord, open my lips, and my mouth will declare your praise.' Rather than growing weary with regret and sorrow because of our sins, we can open our mouths in praise to God.

Prayer: *Gracious God, help us to release our regrets and open our mouths to declare your praise. Amen*

Thought for the day: God's mercy deserves my praise.

Sheryl H. Boldt (Florida, US)

PRAYER FOCUS: TO TURN REGRET INTO PRAISE

Waiting for God

Read Genesis 41:14–16, 39–43
The Lord will fulfil his purpose for me.
Psalm 138:8 (NRSV)

When my father passed away, my neighbours gave me a small orchid to place in the windowsill. At the time it had a beautiful bloom, but the bloom eventually died. My wife and I kept watering the plant and waiting for another bloom. Several years passed; the orchid was alive and green but there was still no bloom. Then one day we noticed a green sprout coming up from the bottom of the plant. Later the sprout showed signs of several buds. One morning a magnificent bloom opened. It was a beautiful sight!

Sometimes I grow impatient waiting for God to act. Then I try to take control because he is not moving in the way that I expect. But God has a purpose for us, one that will be fulfilled according to his plan and timing, not ours.

Many stories in the Bible tell of people waiting for God's action. Joseph, for example, waited years to understand his ultimate purpose; he faced many setbacks and obstacles along the way. But Joseph's patience and unrelenting faith in God carried him through.

As I learned from our orchid, God will produce more than we expect if we continue to trust his timing, not our own.

Prayer: *Dear God, help us to seek you first as we look for direction and guidance. Only you can lead us to our true purpose. Amen*

Thought for the day: I will trust God to act according to his timing.

Brian Foster (North Carolina, US)

Time spent with God

Read Luke 10:38–42
Mary has chosen the better part. It won't be taken away from her.
Luke 10:42 (CEB)

In 2016, I again experienced ill health due to recurrent tuberculosis. Meanwhile my husband was very busy working, and there was tension between my father and me. I resigned from my job to seek treatment for my illness; and while receiving treatment and caring for my family, I also set aside time for God.

I prayed earnestly, devoting myself each day to an hour of prayer and Bible reading. I read the Bible from beginning to end. Through that devotional practice, I grew closer to God and discovered that life is about more than my immediate circumstances.

It has been over a year since that time, and my relationship with God continues to grow. I have experienced physical healing, and my family situation has also improved. Through prayer and reading scripture, I have found the strength to face any situation because I know that God is with me.

Prayer: *Gracious God, thank you for bringing us closer to you. Help us always to seek you and find our hope in you. In the name of Jesus. Amen*

Thought for the day: Scripture reading and prayer can keep me close to God.

Emiriana Malelak-Bana (East Nusa Tenggara, Indonesia)

Employed by God

Read John 14:1–14
We are therefore Christ's ambassadors, as though God were making his appeal through us.
2 Corinthians 5:20 (NIV)

When I woke up, my mind immediately began to replay the events of yesterday. I had met with my boss and handed in my notice of early retirement. In a few weeks I would be without a job.

It had not been done lightly. I had felt the Lord's guidance in making this change, and I had spent a great deal of time in prayer. But now, feelings of loss and nervousness closed in on me. No employment. No reason to leave the house each morning. How would I adapt?

Settling down to my quiet time, I opened my book and read the words: 'Given a job by God. Being anointed means employment by God.'

In a few weeks I will move from worldly employment to God employment. He has guided me to this point in my life and has a job for me to do. He will give me the right mindset, and the ability to adapt and be faithful in what he has planned for me. I feel that life is about to take an exciting turn.

Prayer: *Father God, our daily lives may alter but you never do. We are in your hands. May we look to and trust you in every step of life's journey. Amen*

Thought for the day: We can have no better boss than God.

Julia Cutting (Yorkshire, United Kingdom)

Soaring

Read Isaiah 40:28–31

Those who hope in the Lord will renew their strength. They will soar on wings like eagles; they will run and not grow weary, they will walk and not be faint.
Isaiah 40:31 (NIV)

An eagle is a rare sight where I live. But while my wife and I were kayaking on a glacier lake in Alaska, we spotted as many as 15 eagles. Some were perched in the tops of giant pines along the shoreline. Most were soaring effortlessly far above our heads, searching for fish in the lake below. Buoyed by strong winds beneath their massive outstretched wings, they were lifted to great heights and enabled to fly long distances.

Living a Christian life is much like soaring. We are not to live by our strength alone but are to be carried along by the uplifting power of the Holy Spirit. At times we grow weary. But God's power never diminishes. By his strength, we can be lifted to new spiritual heights to serve him in even greater ways.

God has promised to be with us through life's challenges. We can catch the wind of the Spirit if we pull away from our hectic, crowded days to pray and meditate upon God's word, anticipating the renewing power that our creator offers. Then, empowered by the Holy Spirit, we can rise above life's difficulties, strengthened to meet life's demands.

Prayer: *Dear God, we want to soar to new heights, so we wait for the refreshing, restorative power your Spirit brings. Amen*

Thought for the day: The Spirit enables me to rise above life's challenges.

Wayne Greenawalt (Illinois, US)

From loss to gain

Read Revelation 21:1–4

[God] will wipe away every tear from their eyes. Death will be no more. There will be no mourning, crying, or pain anymore, for the former things have passed away.
Revelation 21:4 (CEB)

The past two years have held sadness and loss for our family. My dad died, I settled my mother into a nursing home and I had to empty and sell their home.

Sitting at Dad's desk, I sorted papers and cried over his once-precise handwriting that had later become so shaky. My heart ached at the sight of Christmas decorations that Mother had so lovingly created. Within a matter of weeks, a lifetime of memories had been boxed, stored, shared or sold.

As I walked through the empty house, loss washed over me like a flood. Yet out of those hollow rooms came a sweet reminder of Jesus' assurance to us: 'In my Father's house are many mansions... I go to prepare a place for you' (John 14:2, KJV). My heart's burden was lifted as I gave thanks that our heavenly home is eternal. We – and our loved ones – can rejoice, knowing that there will be no more loss, tears or parting.

Prayer: *Heavenly Father, thank you for your comfort in times of sadness. Help us to remember that you have overcome our earthly losses with your eternal provision. Amen*

Thought for the day: I can face earthly losses with courage, knowing that I have an eternal home.

Sandra Sullivan (West Virginia, US)

PRAYER FOCUS: THOSE MOVING INTO NURSING HOMES

Starry skies

Read Psalm 8:1–9

When I consider your heavens, the work of your fingers, the moon and the stars, which you have set in place, what is mankind that you are mindful of them, human beings that you care for them?
Psalm 8:3–4 (NIV)

One evening I sat at the table with my twelve-year-old daughter and her friend, as we do almost every Tuesday. Sometimes I read to the girls from the Bible, and on that day I read from Psalm 8. Then we talked about the wonders of our universe: how everything in our galaxy is suspended in massive darkness, how our sun is just one of the billions of stars in the Milky Way and that there are likely many species of plants and animals living on the earth still undiscovered.

While we were discussing God's greatness and power, the sky suddenly turned a beautiful pink. Both girls ran outside to take photos. My eyes filled with tears and my heart with adoration. It was as if God were smiling at us and saying, 'Yes, my children, I am the creator. I have made the heavens for you to wonder at and enjoy.'

That evening we celebrated God's presence in scripture and in nature. Our creator wants to speak to us every day. When we look out of our window or open our Bibles, God is there.

Prayer: *Creator God, thank you for all of the ways you remind us of your presence. Amen*

Thought for the day: The glory of creation reminds me that God cares for me.

Marcela Nwanosike (Lincolnshire, United Kingdom)

Seeking and waiting

Read 1 Kings 19:1–18

But the Lord was not in the wind. After the wind there was an earthquake, but the Lord was not in the earthquake. After the earthquake came a fire, but the Lord was not in the fire. And after the fire came a gentle whisper.
1 Kings 19:11–12 (NIV)

On a cool, sunny day I was walking through wetlands in central Florida. I stopped to watch a blue heron, standing completely still, fishing. Further down the raised wooden walkway, I spotted a white heron, who was also fishing in the pond. Though the blue heron had watched and waited patiently for the fish to come closer, the white heron walked along looking for fish as he moved. These two herons used very different methods, but they both seemed to catch fish.

I'm not a particularly patient person – more the white heron than the blue, I guess. While patience doesn't always come easily to me, patience is a key to listening – both to others and to God. Most mornings, I set aside time to listen patiently to God before the concerns of the day begin. The great blue heron reminds me that patience and stillness are good ways to 'fish' for what God wants me to hear today. But the successful fishing of the white heron also encourages me to look around and actively seek God's wisdom.

Prayer: *Dear Lord, grant us boldness to seek you and patience to wait to hear your gentle whisper. Amen*

Thought for the day: I can seek God's voice and wisdom both in stillness and by actively looking.

John Robbins (Florida, US)

More fruit

Read John 15:1–8

[Jesus said,] 'I am the true vine, and my Father is the gardener. He cuts off every branch in me that bears no fruit, while every branch that does bear fruit he prunes so that it will be even more fruitful.'
John 15:1–2 (NIV)

Branchy green suckers sprouted from the roots of the crab-apple tree in our garden. They stole nutrition and water that the tree's buds needed in order to bloom. Other trees in the neighbourhood bore pink and white flowers, while my tree struggled just to stay green. Because I wanted my tree to flower too, I took the shears and pruned away the harmful branches. I imagined I heard the tree sigh with relief. Within a few days, white buds burst into bloom.

In today's reading, Jesus reminds us that he is the true vine and that God cuts the unfruitful branches from him. Sometimes – out of fear of change, laziness or habit – I stay in a rut that keeps me from following God's will. It's not easy to change behaviour, step away from a situation or move in a new direction. But sometimes God redirects my path and asks me to change what I'm doing in order to serve better and produce more fruit. He wants me to snip away the dead branches in my life to encourage new growth. The Holy Spirit nudges me to make the needed changes in my life so that I can produce fruit for God.

Prayer: *Dear God, help us every day to produce fruit for you by recognising when we need to prune away unfruitful branches in our lives. Amen*

Thought for the day: I can seek God's will for how best to produce good fruit.

Penny Frost McGinnis (Ohio, US)

The door is open

Read Joshua 10:5–15
I know your works. Look, I have set before you an open door, which no one is able to shut.
Revelation 3:8 (NRSV)

As I write this I'm faced with a problem. I have been accepted for study at a Christian university in America, and I was given an academic scholarship. I am confident that God has opened this door. But now that I am trying to enrol, the people who I thought would help me and sign the financial guarantee papers are ignoring me. While this is discouraging, I trust in God. Even though people seem to be against me, I trust that God has opened this door to me and that no one can shut it.

In today's scripture reading, five kings gathered their forces to attack a city that had made peace with the Israelites. Though the obstacles seemed great, the Lord told Joshua, 'Do not fear them, for I have handed them over to you; not one of them shall stand before you' (Joshua 10:8). The Lord fought for Israel and still fights for us today.

When obstacles come our way, we can look up and trust that God, who has begun a good work in us, will bring it to completion. God is faithful, and his mercy endures forever.

Thought for the day: God, who has begun a good work in me, will bring it to completion (see Philippians 1:6).

Prayer: *Dear Lord, thank you for granting us faith that can move mountains. Guide us as we take steps of faith towards the places where you call us. Amen*

Tarupiwa Muzah (Mashonaland East, Zimbabwe)

Always with us

Read Matthew 28:16–20

[Jesus said,] 'Where two or three gather in my name, there am I with them.'
Matthew 18:20 (NIV)

Several years ago my young daughter said to me, 'At Sunday school we talk about Jesus. I wish I could see Jesus.' That evening as I was preparing dinner, I set an extra place at the table. When the family gathered to eat, my daughter noticed the extra place setting and asked, 'Who else is coming?' I told her we were having a very special guest. As we took our seats, I said, 'Our special guest is Jesus.'

In the Bible, Jesus tells us, 'Where two or three gather in my name, there am I with them.' I explained that Jesus is with us always. He is as close to us as if he were sitting next to us. In fact, he is even closer since his love is always in our hearts. That evening, we were all reminded that Jesus is with us wherever we are and wherever we go.

Prayer: *Dear Lord, help us to remember that your presence surrounds us always. We pray as Jesus taught us, 'Our Father which art in heaven, Hallowed be thy name. Thy kingdom come. Thy will be done, as in heaven, so in earth. Give us day by day our daily bread. And forgive us our sins; for we also forgive every one that is indebted to us. And lead us not into temptation; but deliver us from evil.'* Amen*

Thought for the day: Wherever I am, Jesus is there.

(Ms) Dorothy Johnson (Michigan, US)

God's strong love

Read 1 Corinthians 13:1–8

Perfect love drives out fear.

1 John 4:18 (NIV)

Gerry climbed into the bed next to his dying wife and cradled her in his arms. Holding her weakened body he said, 'Pastor, please pray for us.' I had never seen something so brave and so loving. I prayed that God would bless Louise with every possible healing, and I asked God to strengthen Gerry, whose love was bearing the full burden of Louise's suffering and helplessness. Louise died a few days later. That did not end Gerry's burden of love. His children and grandchildren needed his hugs and smiles, and Gerry needed to care for himself. The greater our love, the greater our burden of care.

But God is love (1 John 4:16), and his love is strong. It carries the heaviest of burdens: our sins, our sorrows and all our cries for help. God's love 'bears all things, believes all things, hopes all things, endures all things' (1 Corinthians 13:7, NRSV).

When our burdens threaten to break us, we can pray for the strong love of God. We will see his answers in many ways. Friends arrive at just the right time. Our daily Bible readings open our eyes to the promises of God. An inner calm surprises us, and we sense the presence of our Saviour. We are given a strength we know isn't ours but comes from God's strong love.

Prayer: *Dear God, help us to rely on your love and to show that love to those around us. Amen*

Thought for the day: When my love needs to be stronger, God's love sustains me.

Tony R. Nester (Iowa, US)

Road less travelled

Read Isaiah 26:1–8

You [Lord] will keep in perfect peace those whose minds are steadfast, because they trust in you.
Isaiah 26:3 (NIV)

One evening on my drive home from college, I encountered heavy traffic due to road works, so I reset my satnav and started on a new route. About 30 minutes into my drive the GPS stopped working. There I was, in the middle of the mountains, with no clue how to get home. I knew that I was still at least an hour away.

As I continued to drive with no signal or knowledge of my location, I felt an overwhelming – but unusual – sense of peace. I just drove. I assumed I would end up somewhere familiar or eventually get my GPS back. I have never felt so content in the midst of so much uncertainty. It was a beautiful drive. I took in all that was around me – fields of horses, mountains, waterfalls and so much natural beauty. It would be hard not to see God in such a journey.

While driving that evening, I realised how often the stresses and worries of everyday life distract me from being present to the beauty and joyful moments of life on earth. Sadly, I often miss them. That day was a reminder that our worry can keep us from seeing the fullness of what God provides.

Prayer: *Dear God, when we are overwhelmed with panic, help us to seek your peace. Amen*

Thought for the day: When I give up worrying, I can more fully rely on God.

Eliza Finley (South Carolina, US)

During hard times

Read Genesis 21:8–21

God heard the boy crying, and the angel of God called to Hagar from heaven and said to her, 'What is the matter, Hagar? Do not be afraid; God has heard the boy crying as he lies there.'
Genesis 21:17 (NIV)

Working in the garden one sunny day made the world feel sweet, but the next day the sunny weather was gone. I uprooted weeds with clouds overhead and a heavy heart. I wish all days could be beautiful! Life is like that too – with good and bad times. We never know what each new day will bring, but scripture assures us that even in difficult times, God does not abandon us.

In Genesis 21, Hagar and her son, Ishmael, went through a very difficult time. Sarah couldn't tolerate Hagar and Ishmael anymore, so she told them to leave. They were abandoned in the desert, where Ishmael wailed and wept. He was dehydrated and the two of them had nowhere to go. Hagar was concerned that her boy would die. But the angel of God called to Hagar from heaven, bringing hope. God led Hagar to a well where they found water to drink. Hagar and Ishmael survived and were blessed in the end.

Sometimes life is hard, but God doesn't abandon us during those times. Like Hagar and Ishmael, God sees us and will help us.

Prayer: *Loving God, help us through the crises and tragedies in life. Amen*

Thought for the day: God is working for good during the hard times.

Peter Veugelaers (Wellington, New Zealand)

Being neighbourly

Read Romans 15:1–7

If you see your fellow Israelite's donkey or ox fallen on the road, do not ignore it. Help the owner to get it to its feet.
Deuteronomy 22:4 (NIV)

I had lived in my sheltered housing community for a year, but I am shy and had met few of my neighbours. One rainy afternoon I looked across the street into my neighbour's driveway and saw that the headlights of one of his cars had been left on. I thought, 'Should I go over there, knock on the door and tell him?' I dithered, thinking that he may have intentionally left the lights on. He might be busy or he could resent my intrusion. Yet I knew in my heart that I should tell him. I resolved that despite my timidity, I could do it with God's help. So I put on my coat and crossed the street to the stranger's home.

After a couple of knocks, the man came to the door. Feeling awkward, I blurted out, 'Did you know your car lights are on?' To my surprise, he thanked me profusely. I hurried away feeling much better.

I had been struggling to discern God's guidance in several big decisions. Yet when I felt his urging over this small matter, I resisted. I realised that if I make excuses and give in to my fears, I can't learn to trust God and discover what he wants me to do.

Prayer: *Dear God, help us to trust you in all things, at all times, and to be open to your leading to help our neighbours. Amen*

Thought for the day: God is ready to help me, even in small matters.

April Bogert (New York, US)

Our unbelief

Read Mark 9:14–29

[Jesus said,] 'Everything is possible for one who believes.' Immediately the boy's father exclaimed, 'I do believe; help me overcome my unbelief!'
Mark 9:23–24 (NIV)

In Mark 9, when some of the disciples were unable to heal a boy with an evil spirit, Jesus reassured the father of the boy, who then responded, 'I do believe; help me overcome my unbelief!' What a profound prayer! The desperate man was trying his best to believe, but he knew he needed help. Jesus accepted the father's imperfect belief and healed the boy. Apparently, healing didn't depend on the father's faith, but on Jesus' righteousness.

That's good news for those of us who struggle with belief. Jesus was brutally beaten, crucified and buried. Even after a violent death, on the third day Jesus rose from the dead and appeared to 500 followers. That story is the cornerstone of the Christian faith. But many in the world, even many in the church, may confront that story with an honest prayer: 'Lord, we believe. Help us to overcome our unbelief.'

The good news is that Jesus meets us where we are. His goodness made up for whatever lack of belief the father in Mark 9 had, and it will make up for a lack of belief in us as well. Jesus invites us to come as we are. When we offer ourselves – unbelief and all – he redeems us.

Prayer: *Dear Lord, we do believe in you, but sometimes we doubt. Help us overcome our unbelief. Amen*

Thought for the day: God's goodness covers my weakness.

Kevin Thomas (Alabama, US)

Half-time

Read Romans 12:1–8

We do not lose heart. Though outwardly we are wasting away, yet inwardly we are being renewed day by day.
2 Corinthians 4:16 (NIV)

Several friends of mine are trying to change their jobs. They have sent many letters and CVs out, but most of them have received no reply. A few were invited to interviews, but the positions offered a lower salary and grade. It seems that many employers are looking for new graduates, so the middle-aged are often less-preferred candidates. It is hard for us to secure the same position in another company. A famous TV star in our city says in an ad that age is just a number. Yet, in reality, this number seems to pave the road ahead with more obstacles. Besides challenges in the workplace, our health becomes more fragile, and we more frequently experience the grief of people close to us dying.

I am thankful that God understands this experience. Even though our bodies deteriorate, our spirits and minds can be renewed by scripture, the people God places in our lives and the experiences of God's love we have each day. This can give us the energy to move forwards in faith even as we wait for the day when we will live in eternity with God.

Prayer: *Dear God, help us to feel your comfort and have the courage to move on. Amen*

Thought for the day: God understands my struggles.

Flo Au (Hong Kong, China)

'I lost Granddad!'

Read Isaiah 41:10–13

[God told Joshua,] 'It is the Lord who goes before you. He will be with you; he will not fail you or forsake you. Do not fear or be dismayed.'
Deuteronomy 31:8 (NRSV)

'I lost Granddad!' my two-and-a-half-year-old grandson would say when I left the house to go to work. For the first few years of his life, he and his mother, our daughter, lived with my wife, Lolly, and me. I wanted to be with him as much as I could, and when my work took me away from him, he was worried that he couldn't find me.

That got me to thinking. Isn't it great that our heavenly Father is never 'lost' to us? God never has to leave for a job or to take out the rubbish. We can pray at any time, and God is always there. What a comfort! Earthly fathers and grandfathers may disappoint us or not be near when needed, but God is always present.

Prayer: *Dear Lord, help us to remember your promise always to be with us. Be with those who feel abandoned or lonely. Amen*

Thought for the day: I can never lose God.

Wright Peavy (Georgia, US)

Fruitful

Read Galatians 5:22–26

The fruit of the Spirit is love, joy, peace, patience, kindness, generosity, faithfulness, gentleness, and self-control.
Galatians 5:22–23 (NRSV)

When I was a young girl, my grandmother kept a bowl full of plastic fruit on her coffee table. My sister and I would play a game by taking turns selecting a piece of fruit from the bowl until it was empty. I was always glad when I got to choose first so that I could pick my favourite: the cluster of bright red cherries. Next I would pick the green apple or the purple grapes. My least favourites were the orange and lemon, and we both avoided the funny-looking kiwi.

Recently as I read today's quoted scripture verses, I thought about this childhood game. I wondered whether I sometimes select certain 'fruits' or Christian characteristics over others because they are easier. Do I eagerly reach for joy but avoid choosing patience? Am I relieved when someone else picks generosity so that I don't have to? Although some fruits of the Spirit are more difficult than others, the good news is that we don't have to be adept in all of the characteristics – God asks for perseverance, not perfection. When we abide in Christ, faithfully trying to embrace and practise these characteristics, we can look forward to the good fruit we will bear together.

Prayer: *Loving God, thank you for your patience as we strive to practise the fruit of the Spirit. Help us to persevere, even when we fail. Amen*

Thought for the day: Which fruit of the Spirit will I practise today?

Amy Burling (Florida, US)

Sadness and love

Read John 14:1–6

[Jesus said,] 'Do not let your hearts be troubled. You believe in God; believe also in me. My Father's house has many rooms; if that were not so, would I have told you that I am going there to prepare a place for you?'
John 14:1–2 (NIV)

When Paulette, my wife of 50 years, died suddenly of a heart attack, I was not prepared for the devastation her loss would cause in my life. But I turned to my faith to sustain me through my grief and sorrow.

Although I have missed Paulette so much, I have learned that Jesus suffers with us and the Holy Spirit provides us with comfort. During those times when I cry out in pain and hurt, Jesus shields me and protects me from dwelling on the bad. Wisdom has been passed on to me through this loss, as I learn a new normal for a life without Paulette.

Christ's death on the cross is the beginning of the resurrection story. We can rejoice, knowing that our loved ones are with God in heaven.

Prayer: *Compassionate God, give us strength to endure the pain over the loss of our loved ones and help us find peace in knowing that they are in their heavenly home. Amen*

Thought for the day: 'You, Lord, are a shield around me' (Psalm 3:3).

Gary Dowdy (Tennessee, US)

Priorities

Read Matthew 22:34–40

Strive first for the kingdom of God and his righteousness, and all these things will be given to you as well.
Matthew 6:33 (NRSV)

It can be easy to prioritise many things over God: families, jobs, studies, sports or music. When I was a teenager, I gave a lot of time to things like the cinema, games, music and TV programmes. But when I came to know my Lord Jesus, he reminded me: 'Abhilasha, you are mine. You should give me the first place in your life. When you seek me and my kingdom, you will lack nothing.' Now that I have my priorities in order, I have found this to be true.

God wants to be our priority. Jesus said, 'You shall love the Lord your God with all your heart, and with all your soul, and with all your mind' (Matthew 22:37).

For five years, I taught in a non-Christian school. While I was there, God helped me through many situations. I am now teaching in a Christian mission school where I find it easier to prioritise my relationship with God, and I am able to know him more deeply and glorify his name. God has provided for me in each stage of my life.

Prayer: *Lord Jesus, help us to seek you and your kingdom above all. May we make you the centre of our lives. Amen*

Thought for the day: Today I will make time with God my top priority.

Abhilasha Morris Paul (Uttar Pradesh, India)

Without words

Read Daniel 2:19–23

Trust in the Lord and do good; dwell in the land and enjoy safe pasture. Take delight in the Lord, and he will give you the desires of your heart.
Psalm 37:3–4 (NIV)

My busy life came to a halt when my right hip began to hurt. By the time hip replacement surgery was arranged, I was dependent on a walking frame. I'd never had much pain and was astonished at how quickly I became incapacitated. After surgery a haematoma formed under the incision, and healing that should have taken about four weeks was drawn out for several more. On strong pain medication, I became depressed, certainly not my typical happy and confident self. I reached out to friends, asking for prayers for healing.

One morning a few weeks later, I awoke from a dream with a sense of peace. I remembered being in darkness but surrounded by hundreds of flickering lights. I felt such calm and comfort that my sleepy mind began praising God. Then it came to me that the lights represented all those who were praying for me during this difficult time.

As with Daniel, God may speak to us through dreams. We may sometimes miss out because the message is not delivered in the way we expect. But the closer our relationship to God, sharing time spent talking and listening, the easier it is to hear him – even if it is without words.

Prayer: *Healer of all frailties, show us your mercy as we earnestly seek a closer relationship with you. Amen*

Thought for the day: God can speak to me without words.

Bobbie Smith Bryant (Kentucky, US)

The cards never stopped

Read Lamentations 3:25–33

Though [the Lord] brings grief, he will show compassion, so great is his unfailing love.
Lamentations 3:32 (NIV)

My friend has sent me greetings cards for the past 30 years. She doesn't send just a birthday or a Christmas card; she sends a card for every holiday. She never misses one. But recently tragedy struck and her home burned to the ground; she lost everything she owned. I was sure that her cards would stop coming, at least for a while. But they didn't. Three weeks after the fire, on St Patrick's Day, a card arrived in the post with her usual cheerful greeting and best wishes. I was stunned. With all the turmoil in her life, how could she possibly find the energy to send a message of good cheer? I could think of only one explanation for that kind of resilience – her faith.

My friend is unaware of how deeply her example has enriched my Christian walk. Sending a greetings card may seem trivial. But when you're stripped of a lifetime of possessions within a few hours and you're still able to convey good wishes to others, that's not trivial; that's a significant witness. While I was concentrating on the tragedy of her loss, my friend was clinging to the one thing no one could ever take from her: Jesus Christ and his promise of love. My friend's continuous acts of kindness shine like a beacon in my life, and I am grateful.

Prayer: *Thank you, Lord, for the people who have shaped and strengthened our Christian walk. Help us to be Christlike examples for others. Amen*

Thought for the day: Because of God's power to redeem, no tragedy can destroy my faith.

Trudy K. Snyder (Pennsylvania, US)

God's ways

Read Isaiah 55:6–13

God is not human, that he should lie, not a human being, that he should change his mind. Does he speak and then not act? Does he promise and not fulfil?
Numbers 23:19 (NIV)

The printer for our church's devotional book notified us that we didn't have enough funds for the 1,000 copies we had planned to print. Still sure the book would be published, I took some time to thank God. I had no idea where the money would come from, but I just kept meditating on God's word. At around ten the next morning, a friend sent the exact amount needed to complete the printing. Truly whatever God promises, he will do.

As our reading says, God's ways are different from ours (Isaiah 55:8) so his way of planning might be different from my way. I would have planned to have the printing funds two months earlier, but God chose to supply my need on the very day I needed it. Just when I had exhausted my own ideas, he made a way.

God is always faithful. Whatever he promises will come to pass.

Prayer: *Dear God, help us to believe your word and to see you as our true God in every step we take. Amen*

Thought for the day: I can rely on God's promises.

Oluwasola Jegede (Lagos, Nigeria)

My responsibility

Read James 1:19–27

Everyone should be quick to listen, slow to speak and slow to become angry, because human anger does not produce the righteousness that God desires.
James 1:19–20 (NIV)

Every day when I turn on the news, I see horrific stories of destructive wars, persecution and mass shootings occurring around the world. Not only do these events anger me, but they also tempt me to lose faith in the goodness of humanity. I begin to wonder, 'Why does God let evil harm the lives of so many?'

After I began earnestly praying for peace, God showed me that it is my responsibility to make the world better in whatever ways I can. Instead of allowing the evil of others to form violent thoughts in my mind, I can focus on doing the small things that God asks of me. Instead of resenting those whose lives are spent spreading evil, I can remember that the Lord said, 'Vengeance is mine; I will repay' (Romans 12:19, KJV).

We are all affected in some way by atrocities that occur around the globe. Instead of focusing on the bad in the world and using violence to fight violence, we can focus on our ability to spread love and goodness. We can find comfort in knowing that God's righteousness will be the final word of justice. Now when I become enraged and discouraged by an attack on humanity, I ask, 'What can I do today to spread a little more of God's love?'

Prayer: *God of all humanity, give us the strength to refrain from responding to violence with violence. Help us to trust that, in time, you will bring justice to all situations. Amen*

Thought for the day: What can I do today to spread a little more of God's love?

Cecilia Kammire (North Carolina, US)

Beyond the walls

Read Galatians 6:2–10
As we have opportunity, let us do good to all people, especially to those who belong to the family of believers.
Galatians 6:10 (NIV)

While eating lunch at the airport, I noticed a young soldier a few tables away. I walked over to thank him for his service to our country. I asked where he was headed, hoping to hear, 'I'm going home.' But he answered, 'I'm on my way to Baghdad, sir.'

Then I noticed several people getting ready to board a plane, and I realised that any of those people might be headed to 'war zones' of their own. They could be facing surgery, dreading a visit to the doctor, caring for ageing parents or worrying about their job. What would it be like to ask others where they are headed and then listen carefully to their answers?

God wants the church to be a family who cares for one another. We can care for one another by thanking people for the blessings they bring to our lives and by showing concern for the trials they may be facing. We can look beyond the walls of our church buildings to tell those who are heading into 'war zones' that they are not alone.

Prayer: *Thank you, God, for sustaining us through times of trial. Make us aware of the hurts and needs of those around us, and prompt us to help. In Jesus' name. Amen*

Thought for the day: How is God leading me to respond to the needs of others?

Andy Baker (Tennessee, US)

Being strong?

Read Romans 6:1–11

If we have been united with [Christ] in a death like his, we will certainly also be united with him in a resurrection like his.
Romans 6:5 (NIV)

Our entire community was shocked when three local secondary-school students tragically died in a car accident just days before the end of the school term. I had taught two of the boys and remembered them fondly. Tears streamed down my face as I drove to school the next morning. I prayed for their families, for their friends and for guidance in how to console my students. I didn't want them to see that I had been crying, so before getting out of my car I wiped away my tears in an attempt to appear strong. One of my students passed me in the hall-way and must have noticed my puffy, red eyes. She stopped and quietly said, 'I think you need a hug.' She gave me a hug and together we shed some more tears. Her compassion showed me it was okay to cry.

I learned that being strong in the wake of tragedy doesn't require hiding our sadness. As Christians we know that even in the midst of our distress we can remain strong in the assurance that death is not the end. As we struggle through times of grief, this promise given to us through the death and resurrection of Jesus Christ strengthens us, gives us hope and enables us to persevere.

Prayer: *Thank you, God, for your Son, Jesus Christ, whose resurrection assures us that death is not the end. Amen*

Thought for the day: My strength comes from the Lord.

Jill Allen Maisch (Maryland, US)

Little cloud of hope

Read 1 Kings 18:41–44

The seventh time [Elijah's servant] said, 'Look, a little cloud no bigger than a person's hand is rising out of the sea.'
1 Kings 18:44 (NRSV)

Three years ago, I was diagnosed with burnout, anxiety and severe depression. Formerly a full-time teacher, my days suddenly revolved around visits to my psychiatrist, taking medication and trying to cope with my fears. I felt weak and frustrated, but I was determined to make a full recovery. I prayed and praised God for my deliverance. I believed that I would get well.

Months went by, but I saw little progress. I felt discouraged and wondered if I would ever get better. But I continued to believe that God would heal me. When I started to get severe headaches, I turned to scripture, fasted and kept praying. I imagined myself being well and whole again, and thanked Jesus for the healing I trusted would come.

One day, the headaches suddenly stopped. It was my little cloud of hope – a small but significant sign of loving assurance from God that healing was coming. Since then, I have been getting stronger every day. God pours out great blessings from small beginnings. And it all starts with a little cloud of hope.

Prayer: *Dear God, thank you for sending us little clouds of hope to assure us of your love and blessing. Amen*

Thought for the day: I will trust God and wait expectantly for the change that is coming.

Madeline Twooney (North Rhine-Westphalia, Germany)

The right place

Read Psalm 62:5–8

Trust in [God] at all times, you people; pour out your hearts to him, for God is our refuge.
Psalm 62:8 (NIV)

My wife and I have two large dogs that sleep at the foot of our bed. Twice a week, they wake up with my wife at 4.30 am and accompany her as she gets ready for work. When she has left the house, instead of coming back to bed, the dogs become restless. Seemingly unaware that I'm still lying in bed, they become frantic – scratching at doors and whining loudly. Finally, I whisper their names and invite them to join me. They leap into bed, nestle into place and drift back to sleep.

As children of God, we often act in the same way. Countless events may cause us to feel forgotten or abandoned: divorce, sickness, the loss of a loved one or simply close friends moving away. During times of loneliness, we may forget God's presence and search for comfort in all the wrong places. When we're unable to find solace, our feelings intensify, making it increasingly difficult to hear God's voice.

Today's reading reminds us that God offers the ultimate place of refuge. When we accept his invitation, feelings of loneliness are quickly replaced with an overwhelming sense of acceptance and comfort. Spending time with God can restore our sense of belonging. There, in God's presence, we can find the blessing of true peace.

Prayer: *Heavenly Father, thank you for always providing a place of comfort and refuge. Help us to remember your presence in times of loneliness. Amen*

Thought for the day: God is my greatest source of comfort.

Webb Smith (Georgia, US)

A fitting title

Read Judges 6:11–16

When the angel of the Lord appeared to Gideon, he said, 'The Lord is with you, mighty warrior.'
Judges 6:12 (NIV)

Mighty warrior. What a strange greeting! The title didn't seem to fit Gideon at all. He did not look like a brave hero. He looked more like a frightened farmer. He was threshing wheat in secret to hide it from invaders. Fearful and discouraged, he was convinced that the Lord had abandoned his people. Even more, Gideon considered himself the least important person in his family. How could he possibly be called a mighty warrior? And how could the Lord trust him with the task of rescuing God's people?

Meditating on this story, I can understand Gideon's reluctance to accept the lofty title and task. It's easy for me to feel similarly unqualified when God calls me 'ambassador for Christ' and trusts me with the ministry of reconciliation (see 2 Corinthians 5:19–20). Who am I to bear such a lofty title and task?

But the promise of God's constant presence is what allows us to fill the role and live up to that title. 'The Lord is with you,' said the angel to Gideon. 'I am with you always,' says Christ to his ambassadors (Matthew 28:20). Christ's empowering presence qualifies us to do God's work in the world.

Prayer: *Dear Lord Jesus, with the sure promise of your presence, we serve gladly as your ambassadors. Amen*

Thought for the day: Christ empowers me to do God's work in the world.

Marion Speicher Brown (Florida, US)

Forwards in hope

Read Isaiah 43:1–3

Do not fear, for I am with you; do not be dismayed, for I am your God.
I will strengthen you and help you; I will uphold you with my righteous
right hand.
Isaiah 41:10 (NIV)

One morning on my walk to work, I saw a little bird walking on the pavement. I could not help slowing down to gaze at it. Then the bird started to walk towards the road, which was filled with buses and trucks. I was alarmed and blocked its way ahead. It flew a short distance and then continued walking towards the road. I quickly blocked it again. It tweeted and flew to a branch nearby, looking at me reproachfully.

I was relieved that it had not been run over by a car, but that look reminded me that I can sometimes behave like the bird. At times I have attempted to move ahead, following my own dreams and desires, but obstacles block my path. In such times, like the tweets of that bird, I complain to God, asking why my way has been blocked. But when I look back on those times, I realise that each obstacle had a purpose. They led me to where I am today. God has always been protecting me. Even when we experience difficulties or obstacles, we do not have to worry. We can walk on with hope in our hearts, knowing that God is with us.

Prayer: *Heavenly Father, thank you for your great love. Forgive us when we try to move ahead without you. Help us to follow Jesus' example as we pray, 'Yet not as I will, but as you will' (Matthew 26:39). Amen*

Thought for the day: When the way closes ahead of me, God will uphold me.

Hisako Adachi (Kanagawa, Japan)

Orchids for Carolyn

Read Psalm 105:1–6

You will seek the Lord your God, and you will find him if you search after him with all your heart and soul.
Deuteronomy 4:29 (NRSV)

After my heart transplant, I began taking time to slow down and reflect on the little miracles that happen in our everyday lives. Just after my operation, my mum asked me what I wanted when I came home. I told her that I wanted an orchid. I felt a new desire to learn about orchids and to take care of something while I was healing at home. I arrived home to find a beautiful purple orchid from my mother. I learned how to care for it, and it made me smile.

The following year, I received a letter from my heart donor's brother, and we started chatting over the next few months. I learned that Carolyn, my heart donor, had saved the lives of several people by donating her organs. I told her brother that on Carolyn's birthday I planned to put flowers in my church in her memory. He replied that Carolyn had loved flowers, especially orchids, which she had grown in her garden.

At that moment we knew: God and Carolyn were sending us a little sign that all was well. It is almost three years since my heart transplant, and I still collect orchids in memory of Carolyn. Every day during this second chance at life that God and Carolyn have given me, I watch for the little signs of God all around.

Prayer: *Heavenly Father, when we see no way through our trials, help us to have faith in you and to trust your guidance. Amen*

Thought for the day: If I remain alert, I can see little miracles every day.

Dayna Nestor (Pennsylvania, US)

The carpenter

Read 2 Corinthians 5:16–21

Therefore, if anyone is in Christ, the new creation has come: the old has gone, the new is here!
2 Corinthians 5:17 (NIV)

I have a tiny woodworking shop in the basement of my house, and I love spending time making things. One day I was planing down a rough piece of oak timber and marvelling at how, with just a bit of scraping on the surface, an unattractive piece of wood can become so beautiful. Wood that starts out rough and unremarkable can become smooth to the touch and reveal the intricate patterns of its grain. As a woodworker, you look at wood differently – you don't just see timber; you see what it can become in your hands.

I then realised that our Saviour, Jesus Christ, was a carpenter and probably understood this experience. As a woodworker looks at timber, Jesus sees each of us – not just who we are but who we can become. Before we meet Jesus, we are like a rough piece of timber. But the carpenter planes away our sin, sanding and shaping us with gentle and loving hands until we become beautiful.

Prayer: *Lord Jesus, shape us into beautiful masterpieces, ready to do your work. Open our eyes to see the beauty in those around us. Amen*

Thought for the day: In Jesus' hands, I become a masterpiece.

Miles Q. Turner (Illinois, US)

A beautiful blessing

Read John 17:13–26

[Jesus prayed,] 'My prayer is not for them alone. I pray also for those who will believe in me through their message.'
John 17:20 (NIV)

At our wedding reception, a friend of my grandparents who had known me my whole life hugged me. She told me how proud my mother would have been of me. I appreciated that connection to the past – especially since my mother and grandparents are no longer alive.

I was surprised, however, when her husband also hugged me and took my hand. I could not recall ever having a conversation with him, yet he said, 'I've been praying for you since you were a little girl.' Nothing any other guest had said to me was as meaningful as that. I had spent my life unaware of this man, yet he had cared enough to pray for me all this time. I was grateful for this beautiful blessing.

Before Jesus was betrayed and crucified, he prayed for us. First he prayed that his disciples would be protected in their faith and that they would be made holy. He entrusted God's message to them to share with others as Jesus had shared it with them. He then prayed for all who would believe because of their message. That's us!

In the body of Christ, we are all family. We can show our love by praying for one another.

Prayer: *Heavenly Father, help us to see others through your eyes and with your love. Soften our hearts to the needs of others, and remind us to pray for them. Amen*

Thought for the day: Today I will tell someone that I am praying for them.

Melinda VanRy (New York, US)

Comfort and hope

Read Psalm 34:1–8

Happy are those who take refuge in [the Lord].
Psalm 34:8 (NRSV)

Many years ago, after a walk in the park, my children and I were going home. Unexpectedly, my younger daughter tore her hand from mine and ran out into the street directly into the path of a car. In a moment, I felt that my whole life was broken. I closed my eyes and asked God, 'Why?' I dreaded the thought of looking underneath that car.

When I did, I thanked God that it was not as bad as I had feared. My daughter had fallen between the wheels, and the driver had been driving slowly. To my surprise, the driver came to the hospital the next day to say he was sorry, despite the fact that it was not his fault.

To this day, I give thanks to my Lord for protecting my child. Reading the Bible regularly has shown me that we can seek God not only when we face difficulties and fear but in every situation, good or bad. God's word in scripture gives me comfort and hope for my life's journey.

Prayer: *Thank you, God, for your caring love every day, not only in the most terrifying moments of our lives but in joyful times as well. Help us to trust you and to have thankful hearts. Amen*

Thought for the day: Whether I am fearful or joyful, God is with me.

Volya Koruderlieva (Varna, Bulgaria)

Not much fun?

Read Revelation 22:1–5

'What no eye has seen, what no ear has heard, and what no human mind has conceived'– the things God has prepared for those who love him – these are the things God has revealed to us by his Spirit.
1 Corinthians 2:9–10 (NIV)

Growing old isn't as much fun as I had imagined. Being retired is good. But my knees don't work as well as they used to, my aching back wakes me up too early some mornings and I can't run the way I did as a young man. Is there any fun in growing old? The answer seems to depend on what I focus on.

That may be one reason Paul tells us to 'set your minds on things above' (Colossians 3:2). The apostle shared a glimpse of heaven when he wrote that we 'will be caught up together with [the dead in Christ] in the clouds to meet the Lord in the air. And so we will be with the Lord forever' (1 Thessalonians 4:17). When we let God's word guide our imagination, we can gain a new perspective on life and eternal life. How exciting it is to imagine seeing Jesus as he really is, to look into the face of the one who loves us with an everlasting love! How exciting to think of being more like him than we've ever been before!

Focusing on our eternal home can change not only the way we think but also the way we act and how we treat others. Growing older can be an exciting experience when we focus our minds on things above and the life that awaits us.

Prayer: *Dear Lord Jesus, fill us with your thoughts so that we can see everyone in our lives as you do. Amen*

Thought for the day: Focusing on things above can change my perspective.

Dave Caswell (Arkansas, US)

The best example

Read 1 Peter 2:18–24

When they hurled their insults at [Christ], he did not retaliate; when he suffered, he made no threats. Instead, he entrusted himself to him who judges justly.
1 Peter 2:23 (NIV)

Recently I left a job in which I was treated unfairly by the management. Just before I left, I received information that could have caused problems for the leaders of the organisation. I struggled with the temptation to use this information to repay them for the wrong they had done me.

During this time, I read about the death of Jesus and his response to those who crucified him: 'Father, forgive them, for they do not know what they are doing' (Luke 23:34). This made me ask myself: 'If Jesus could forgive and have understanding towards those who persecuted him, how much more should I extend the same response to those who treated me unfairly?' Once I looked at my situation from that perspective, my desire for revenge disappeared. My situation seemed trivial when compared to that of Jesus, and yet he had responded with compassion and understanding for his enemies.

Following Jesus' example, I made up my mind to forgive, and I began to feel peace about my situation. I no longer felt weighed down by the desire for revenge. This lesson taught me to view my own experiences through the eyes of our Saviour and to seek his example for how to respond.

Prayer: *Dear heavenly Father, when we are tempted to seek revenge, help us to see the world through your eyes and to follow your Son's example. Amen*

Thought for the day: Jesus is the ultimate example of forgiveness.

Heidi Kling-Newnam (Pennsylvania, US)

Patient with us

Read 2 Peter 3:1–9

The Lord is compassionate and gracious, slow to anger, abounding in love.
Psalm 103:8 (NIV)

As a schoolteacher, I learn a lot as I try to impart knowledge and sound moral training to my young pupils. The greatest lesson I believe I can share is that of patience. I have developed patience over time as I try to teach particular subjects or topics that the children seem slow to understand.

As children of God, we should remember that the Father has much to teach us. Yet God knows our weaknesses and is patient and loving in teaching us. Jesus was patient with Peter; despite Peter's failings, Jesus forgave him and gave him the privilege of leadership in God's kingdom.

Just as teachers and pupils must share a trusting relationship in order to foster the learning process, it is very important for us to know that God cares about us. He helps us to overcome our daily challenges as we grow in our walk with Christ.

Prayer: *Dear God, help us to be patient and to trust your care for us as we learn your purpose for us. 'Father, hallowed be your name, your kingdom come. Give us each day our daily bread. Forgive us our sins, for we also forgive everyone who sins against us. And lead us not into temptation.'* Amen*

Thought for the day: God is patient with me and encourages me to be patient with others.

Joshua Oladipupo (Lagos, Nigeria)

PRAYER FOCUS: GRATITUDE FOR GOD'S PATIENCE WITH ME
*Luke 11:2–4

Remember me

Read Luke 18:15–17
Jesus called the children to him and said, 'Let the little children come to me, and do not hinder them, for the kingdom of God belongs to such as these.'
Luke 18:16 (NIV)

My young grandson, Luka, and I settled into our seats in church on Good Friday. As the service began, we gazed up at the large bare cross near the altar. Various people read scripture or shared prayers concerning this most holy season. The mood was sombre. After each prayer the congregation sang, 'Jesus, remember me when you come into your kingdom.' Luka listened intently and sang vigorously. After the fourth time of singing this refrain Luka substituted these words: 'Jesus, remember Luka when you come into your kingdom.' I stopped singing and tears welled up in my eyes.

God gave Luka an understanding that many adults have yet to comprehend – his love and grace are available to us all; we have only to respond.

Prayer: *Loving God, your grace truly is sufficient for us. When we forget, forgive us and continue to shower your love on us. Amen*

Thought for the day: Even when I am struggling, Jesus remembers me.

Selina Inabinet Duncan (Tennessee, US)

The hope of Easter

Read Matthew 28:1–10
So we fix our eyes not on what is seen, but on what is unseen, since what is seen is temporary, but what is unseen is eternal.
2 Corinthians 4:18 (NIV)

On the Saturday before Easter I woke up in tears, feeling completely overwhelmed. I had given up a well-paid job that enabled me to live a life dedicated to ministry, and now, in my new vocation, my path was riddled with obstacles. To make matters worse, my husband had just been told that the promotion he had been promised had been given to someone else. We couldn't understand why God felt so far off and silent. We were anxious and confused.

I realised how disoriented the disciples must have felt on the Saturday before the first Easter. They not only mourned the loss of their teacher and friend, but also their hopes and dreams that he would be their earthly king. Their decision to leave their jobs and families to follow Christ must have seemed pointless, and they must have been confused and looking for answers.

Like the disciples, we can't always see how God is working in our lives. But we know how the story ends. Amid the confusion, anxiety and waiting we may experience during our 'Saturday', we can be assured that God is at work in the world, giving us the hope of Sunday – the resurrection of Easter morning – and new life through Christ.

Prayer: *Dear Lord, we pray for those who are going through a 'Saturday' – those who are in a time of confusion and waiting. Give us the hope of Easter Sunday. Amen*

Thought for the day: Even when I can't see it, God is working in my life.

Erica Smith (Tennessee, US)

Beyond the thorns

Read Philippians 3:7–11
Through [Christ] you believe in God, who raised him from the dead and glorified him, and so your faith and hope are in God.
1 Peter 1:21 (NIV)

It was Easter time. I was planting a new rose bush when I snagged my finger on one of its many thorns. With greater care and more watchful of the thorns, I separated the bush's stems to discover the first swelling buds. For me, this bush was a message about Easter. Looking beyond the thorns, we can fix our eyes on new life and the hope of beauty to come.

The same is true of our personal experiences of pain and sorrow. We may be pricked by the thorns of questions, doubts and uncertainties, but we hold on to God's promises. That's faith. At the same time, we keep looking for the buds of new life. That's hope.

With hope and faith, our pain and suffering will end in new life. That is God's promise at Easter.

Prayer: *Dear Lord, increase in us faith for today and hope for tomorrow. Amen*

Thought for the day: Faith in Christ Jesus sustains me now. Hope in him leads me to resurrection.

Colin Harbach (Cumbria, United Kingdom)

Never lost

Read Psalm 16:5–11

I keep my eyes always on the Lord. With him at my right hand, I shall not be shaken.
Psalm 16:8 (NIV)

Cumin, curry and Ethiopian berbere spices mingled with wood-fire smoke and dust in my nostrils; bartering voices and foreign words filled my ears at Mercato in Addis Ababa, one of the largest open-air markets in Africa. The beautiful colours, faces and smiles around me became a nightmare as my young son's hand slipped out of mine. I frantically searched for him as fear crept over me. But then, my eyes locked on to the back of his bright-red shirt a mere ten feet away. Two friendly Oromo women had waved him over so they could touch his blonde hair and stare into his blue eyes.

Quickly covering the distance, I cried, 'Son! I thought I had lost you!' Tears edged my voice. 'Mummy, you always know where I am,' he confidently replied. What faith he had in me!

Sometimes we move away from God and wonder if he has lost track of us. But God never leaves us or forsakes us, and he always knows where we are. No matter what, we can have faith knowing that God will always find us.

Prayer: *Father God, help us to keep our eyes focused on you. Thank you for never letting us go. Amen*

Thought for the day: When I hold God's hand, I can never get lost.

Leigh Mackenzie (Illinois, US)

In everything

Read Colossians 3:12–17
Whatever you do, whether in word or deed, do it all in the name of the Lord Jesus, giving thanks to God the Father through him.
Colossians 3:17 (NIV)

Whether we are at home or at work, most of us have a to-do list of tasks that must be done. Though necessary, they are often tedious and certainly not fun. But the way we accomplish them is just as important as completing them. Do we have a positive attitude? Are we thankful for the health and ability to do these things? Or are we negative, performing these tasks with minimal effort?

In today's verse, Paul encourages us to do everything in the name of the Lord. In another letter, he states that we are to be workers who don't need to be ashamed (see 2 Timothy 2:15). 1 Corinthians 13 is also quite specific about the love we should show in everything we do.

Mowing the lawn and housework are two chores I find tedious, but when I view them in the light of Paul's words, I can be grateful for the blessing of owning and maintaining a home and garden. When other people see me working joyfully, they may ask why, and I can take that opportunity to share the gospel message.

Prayer: *Heavenly Father, thank you for our ability to serve. Even when we're doing things we don't want to do, help us to reflect your joy to others. Amen*

Thought for the day: I may be the only image of Christ that others will see today.

Doug Brady (Alabama, US)

PRAYER FOCUS: TO SERVE GOD WITH ALL MY MIGHT

Living with the scars

Read 2 Corinthians 12:7b–10

Gladly therefore will I rather glory in my infirmities, that the power of Christ may rest upon me.
2 Corinthians 12:9 (KJV)

Whenever my life takes a rough turn, I often dwell not only on the current source of my frustration but also on the challenges I have faced in the past. During one of those difficult times, the lines from a song about how we have to live with our scars came to mind. I thought to myself, 'I have so many scars already!'

At that moment, God reminded me of something I learned in an immunology class. Scar formation is a natural part of the healing process. An injury does not become a scar until the wound has completely healed. If a scar is forming, the wound is healing.

I understood that I could choose to view my scars either as reminders of the hurt I had experienced or as reminders of how God had stepped into situations of brokenness and destruction and set me on the path of healing, igniting hope in a situation of despair.

I can look at my scars and remember either the pain and sorrow or the faithfulness and unchanging love of God, who has the power to redeem and renew, transform and restore.

Prayer: *Jesus, our wounded healer, remind us that you understand our suffering and have the power to make us new. Amen*

Thought for the day: I will praise God, who has redeemed and restored me.

Muriella Alexander (Maharashtra, India)

Turbulence

Read Matthew 8:23–27
*The [disciples] were amazed and asked, 'What kind of man is this?
Even the winds and the waves obey him!'*
Matthew 8:27 (NIV)

When I was ten years old, I went on my first plane ride and fell asleep during the flight. To my surprise the landing was a bit rocky. I awoke in a panic and grabbed my father's arm, feeling sure that we were going to die. He took my hand and said, 'It's okay. We have arrived.' I breathed a sigh of relief, marvelled at my first view of the city and anticipated the adventure ahead.

When I remember my experience, I wonder if that is how the disciples felt in today's reading. The seas were rough and Jesus was asleep. When they woke Jesus, he stilled their fears – much like my father did for me in that plane – and then Jesus calmed the storm. The disciples were in awe at what Jesus had done.

At times we may feel that everything around us is in disarray. We may be confused, disappointed or discouraged. Even when we feel as if we are on the brink of perishing, we can find comfort when we remember that Jesus is with us and will see us through the storm. When life feels turbulent, we do not need to fear. We can call on Jesus, who can still whatever seems unsteady.

Prayer: *Dear Lord, help us to hold on to you when life gets shaky. Remind us to call on you during the storm. Amen*

Thought for the day: When life gets rocky, I will call on Jesus.

Adrienne Rayfield (South Carolina, US)

Faith

Read Genesis 15:5 15

Jesus told [Thomas], 'Because you have seen me, you have believed;
blessed are those who have not seen and yet have believed.'
John 20:29 (NIV)

I thought I knew well the story of God's promise to Abram from today's reading – that his descendants would be as numerous as the stars in the sky. Yet I had not really considered the rest of the passage. God told Abram to look up at the sky and count the stars in the heavens 'if you are able to' (v. 5, NRSV). I always assumed that this took place at night, but after the words and events of the next seven verses we read, 'As the sun was going down, a deep sleep fell upon Abram' (v. 12). This made me wonder if it was broad daylight when God asked Abram to look up at the sky. If so, Abram would not have been able to see any stars, which would underscore the extent of faith and trust that the Lord was asking of him. Just as the stars were present but invisible at that moment, so God was asking Abram to have faith even when the fulfilment wasn't evident. Abram was willing to fully commit to God's plan for him.

How often do I expect my prayers to be answered when I want, rather than in God's good time? God's timing differs from ours as we are being brought along the path that he has laid before us. Our path forwards may not be easy or clearly visible, but we can trust our loving God to keep his promises.

Prayer: *Faithful God, help us to trust that you will fulfil your promises and to walk faithfully with you. Amen*

Thought for the day: I will trust God with my future.

Kurt Elward (Virginia, US)

Delight

Read Psalm 34:3–7

This poor man called, and the Lord heard him; he saved him out of all his troubles.
Psalm 34:6 (NIV)

When I was small I used to sit on my father's lap, and he would tell me the story of the old man who was walking along with his head in the air. He wasn't looking where he was going and suddenly he fell into a big hole. When he reached this point my father would open his knees so that I started to fall off his lap. I shrieked with excitement because I knew I was entirely safe; although it seemed that I was falling, my father still had hold of me and would not let me be harmed.

I was reminded of this the other day. I felt that I had fallen into a pit of depression. I used to suffer from this in the past, but over many years I have been learning to claim the Lord as my strength and my song. But here I was – a sudden attack from Giant Despair and I felt like I was again at the bottom of the pit. Then God gently reminded me that just as my earthly father would never have let me fall, my heavenly Father holds me safe in his keeping and I need not fear.

God enabled me to call to him; once again he answered me and delivered me from all my fears.

Prayer: *Dear Lord, help us to trust in you even at times of depression and fear. Amen*

Thought for the day: My heavenly Father holds me safe.

Pauline Lewis (South Wales, United Kingdom)

The risen Christ

Read John 20:11–22
When the disciples were together, with the doors locked for fear of the Jewish leaders, Jesus came and stood among them and said, 'Peace be with you!'
John 20:19 (NIV)

In September 1981, the church building in Sandnes, Norway, reopened after several weeks of being closed. While I was serving as minister, the church received a donation that allowed the church council to commission a new altar icon.

After taking part in our worship services for several weeks, the artist, Per Odd Aarrestad, withdrew to his workshop to start creating. The result – a carved wooden relief of the risen Christ – was stunning. At the reopening, the artist gave a short speech: 'Before I could start working on the relief, I needed to feel the spirit in this congregation,' he said. 'I realised that this church needed a picture of the risen Christ in front of the now-empty cross where he had been crucified three days earlier.' The artist had depicted an important truth: the crucified Jesus is now the risen Christ who is with us every day.

Prayer: *Almighty God, thank you for enfolding us with your limitless love and concern. We praise you for sending us your Son and for giving us new life. Amen*

Thought for the day: How can I reflect the love of Christ today?

Øystein Brinch (Oslo, Norway)

Restoration

Read Psalm 23:1–6

Restore to me the joy of your salvation and grant me a willing spirit, to sustain me.
Psalm 51:12 (NIV)

It's been more than three years since my husband died at the age of 54. I thought I'd be better by now – with counselling, time and serving in my church. But my sorrow and grief linger like uninvited guests who won't leave.

To help reconcile my grief and find purpose, I have been collecting old, broken furniture and restoring it. Then, using words and photos clipped from recycled magazines, I decoupage the furniture, giving it a new life. This process has allowed me time to think, pray and see that there is still beauty in all things, even in the brokenness of my heart.

Slowly I am finding small windows of joy, reminding me that God is with me. He is the joy of my salvation, and he values and loves all of me, even the broken parts. Grief can rob us of many things, but it doesn't have to rob us of God's joy that enables us to walk through deep valleys.

Prayer: *God of joy, remind us of our beauty in times when we feel vulnerable and fragile. Guide us to be hands of healing to those experiencing difficulties, and give us a song of joy to sing even as we cry. In Jesus' name. Amen*

Thought for the day: God is the joy of my salvation.

Malinda Dunlap Fillingim (North Carolina, US)

Strength from solitude

Read Mark 1:35–39

[Jesus] said to [the apostles], 'Come with me by yourselves to a quiet place and get some rest.'
Mark 6:31 (NIV)

I love my job as a teacher, but it is quite demanding. All day I deal with students' needs and questions: 'May I get some water?' 'May I go to the bathroom?' 'I don't understand number three.' Between classes, I have meetings, parents' evenings and endless preparation. It is an honour to teach, but sometimes I need a few quiet moments to myself to say a prayer or to think and refocus.

Some people do not enjoy being alone, but a little solitude can provide an opportunity to reconnect with our spiritual life. Jesus asked the disciples to come away with him to rest and to escape the crowds. He knew that solitude would renew them.

Jesus was a healer and also a teacher. As he travelled and taught, the crowds were relentless in following him, asking him to teach, perform miracles and heal. He used solitude to talk to God and renew his strength.

Solitude is not something to be dreaded or feared. It is an important time to rest, pray and renew our spirits. As Jesus said, 'Come with me… and get some rest.'

Prayer: *Dear God, thank you for moments of solitude to connect with you. May we seek such moments often. Amen*

Thought for the day: Where can I find solitude to reconnect with God today?

Sharon Wright Mitchell (Georgia, US)

Not about us

Read Numbers 11:21–30

A young man ran and told Moses, 'Eldad and Medad are prophesying in the camp.' Joshua son of Nun, who had been Moses' assistant since youth, spoke up and said, 'Moses, my lord, stop them!'
Numbers 11:27–28 (NIV)

Most of us have probably heard the saying 'Be good, and I'll give you a treat.' Sometimes we think about God in much the same way – that God will give us favours in return for our good deeds. However, scripture teaches that our good deeds and good behaviour will not change God's character or influence his choices. We do not need to impress God to gain his grace.

In today's scripture reading, Eldad and Medad clearly did not follow orders to go out to the tent, but God's Spirit rested on them and they prophesied. At times we react like Joshua when we see what God is doing through people like Eldad or Medad, who do not seem to be following God's will. But in those moments, we can remember that it is about God, not us. God can work through anyone for his purpose. That's not an invitation to live in any manner we choose or simply to wait passively for the Lord's blessing. Instead, it is assurance that it is not our performance but our willingness to fulfil God's purpose that he desires.

Prayer: *Almighty God, rest your Spirit on us and grant us the wisdom to trust in the plans you have for us. Make us willing to fulfil your purpose for our lives. Amen*

Thought for the day: God does not choose me based on my behaviour.

David Garcia Escobar (Valle del Cauca, Colombia)

Changing my prayer

Read 2 Kings 5:1–15

Elisha sent a messenger to say to [Naaman], 'Go, wash yourself seven times in the Jordan, and your flesh will be restored and you will be cleansed.'

2 Kings 5:10 (NIV)

The story of Naaman – a leper – reminds me of myself years ago. When I was a young adult, I had a poor relationship with my father. For years I prayed earnestly that God would show him the many faults I found with him. I was angry and hurt, and it was the only perspective I could see.

After years of praying with no visible change in my father, it occurred to me that perhaps I was praying the wrong prayer. I began asking God to change me and to give me a forgiving heart. What had happened with my dad wasn't going to change. It was over and done with. I wanted to move on but sensed that I would not see an improvement in our relationship unless I began this new prayer.

The answer finally came. My heart was changed, and I forgave. This allowed a relationship to grow. It wasn't a grand, quick miracle any more than Naaman received a miracle before he had completely followed Elisha's instructions. But the right attitude and following God's direction resulted in a similar outcome. Just as God healed Naaman, God healed my heart.

Prayer: *Dear God, help us to look to you for guidance and to recognise and accept your guidance when it comes. Amen*

Thought for the day: I can pray for God to change my heart.

Margie J. Harding (Maryland, US)

PRAYER FOCUS: PARENTS AND CHILDREN WITH BROKEN RELATIONSHIPS   123

Terminal

Read 2 Corinthians 4:11—5:4

Always be prepared to give an answer to everyone who asks you to give the reason for the hope that you have.
1 Peter 3:15 (NIV)

It had been two years since I'd heard the oncologist describe my painful cancer as incurable. I felt as if I were riding on prayers as my friends, family and church community surrounded me with their love and support. The staff at the cancer centre became like family to me when I paid my monthly visits there.

As I was taking the hospital bus to the cancer centre, a distraught young woman sat beside me. She talked about her recent cancer diagnosis, and I tried to encourage her by sharing some of my own story. She asked me how I could speak so joyously and positively, knowing that I had a terminal disease. I shared my faith with her – that I know life on this present earth isn't all there is for me.

Through my experience with cancer, I have come to realise that everyone is terminal; no one knows when their last day on earth will be. Every person, healthy or ill, can choose to see each day God gives as a gift.

I know where I am headed. I know God holds my future and I trust him to prepare me for whatever comes.

Prayer: *Heavenly Father, thank you for your promises that give us hope. Amen*

Thought for the day: Every day I will live life to the fullest and for the glory of God.

Anita Gray (Pennsylvania, US)

Safely home

Read Psalm 119:105–112

Thy word is a lamp unto my feet and a light unto my path.
Psalm 119:105 (KJV)

On the way home after a walk, I became disoriented and got lost. Because I am blind, I relied on the position of the sun and on directions from my talking compass to find my way home. Raised bumps on pavements indicating a kerb also helped me orient myself. Once I got these marks fixed in mind and under my feet, I resumed my walk. By God's grace, I got home safely.

Just as I relied on my compass and raised bumps to guide me, we all need God's word to guide our steps as we face challenges and obstacles. Reading and meditating on the word of God will guide us through whatever we encounter, and we can share this gift of the gospel to help others find their way.

Prayer: *Dear God, help us to focus on your word and your grace as we face life's challenges. We pray the prayer Jesus taught us, 'Our Father in heaven, hallowed be your name, your kingdom come, your will be done, on earth as it is in heaven. Give us today our daily bread. And forgive us our debts, as we also have forgiven our debtors. And lead us not into temptation, but deliver us from the evil one.'* Amen*

Thought for the day: The gospel guides me on my way.

Roger Brannon (Florida, US)

*Matthew 6:9–13 (NIV)

Never alone

Read John 14:15–31

[Jesus said to his disciples,] 'I will not leave you as orphans; I will come to you.'
John 14:18 (NIV)

My father showed symptoms that we feared meant he had suffered a stroke. I suddenly had a terrifying thought. What if my father died? I felt that my life would be very difficult if I had to live without my father. Among other concerns, I wondered what would happen to my older brother, who suffers from mental illness. My father was his daily carer, and I wondered if my sister and I were ready to take on that role.

Yet John 14:18 reassures me that God will never leave me alone. Just before Jesus was taken up to heaven, he asked the Father to give us an advocate to help us and be with us forever. Once I realised that I am never left alone, I felt the heavy burden slowly disappear.

My earthly father has limitations, but my heavenly Father is limitless. Even when my earthly father goes home to heaven someday, I can remember that my heavenly Father has promised not to leave me as an orphan. And God is trustworthy.

Prayer: *Loving God, whenever we feel alone in our struggles, help us to remember that you are always with us. Amen*

Thought for the day: Whatever the future brings, God will be there to give me strength.

Linawati Santoso (East Java, Indonesia)

The finish line

Read 2 Timothy 4:1–8

I have fought the good fight, I have finished the race, I have kept the faith.
2 Timothy 4:7 (NRSV)

My son loves to run. He spends hours and hours after school running in our rural community – across miles of terrain that changes from asphalt streets to roughly packed gravel to paths through golden fields where cows graze nearby.

Last year his college cross-country team went to the California State Championships to compete with runners from all over the state. As I stood at the finish line, the first runner to cross was way ahead of the others. Finally, the rest of the racers crossed – some in groups of two or three and others in packs. Then I saw my son run down the last stretch in second-to-last place. He worked so hard to get over the finish line.

It was when I saw those last runners that I realised how we tend to discount the dedication of those who finish last. We look at the place-ment of the runners as the sign of their dedication, not at their perse-verance in finishing the race. Today's reading tells us it's about finishing the race faithfully, not where we are when we cross the finish line. Our crossing the finish line pleases God.

Prayer: *Gracious God, thank you for strength to persevere when the race of our lives wearies us. We look to you to keep us moving on. Amen*

Thought for the day: It's not where I finish but that I finish that counts to God.

Sarah Lunsford (California, US)

Trust during healing

Read Psalm 118:5–9

Trust in the Lord forever, for in the Lord God you have an everlasting rock.
Isaiah 26:4 (NRSV)

I recently had two operations just six weeks apart to remove large kidney stones from both my kidneys. Following each operation, I bemoaned the days I lost, unable to focus at home on reading, writing or even watching television.

But those days had a different purpose in God's plan: developing my ability to trust. I had to trust the surgeon, the operating theatre staff and the nurses. After my operation I had to trust my family who helped to care for me at home, the instructions and medication I was given, and the medical recommendations about when to remove the painful drainage tubes from my back. Most importantly, I had to trust that I was placed firmly in God's hands.

Now that my incisions have healed and I have returned to health, my pain is gone. The days after my operations were not wasted or lost. They taught me to trust God with my life and health. I now know that I will never be disappointed by God's presence and care.

Prayer: *Gracious God, help us to appreciate our times of rest and healing as gifts of grace and not just burdens that we have to bear. Renew our strength. Amen*

Thought for the day: God's presence and loving care will never disappoint me.

John R. Robinson (Georgia, US)

Open my eyes

Read Matthew 20:29–34

Open my eyes, so that I may behold wondrous things out of your law.
Psalm 119:18 (NRSV)

When Jesus was passing by, the two blind men sitting by the road cried out to him. When Jesus asked, 'What do you want me to do for you?' (Matthew 20:32), they answered, 'Lord, let our eyes be opened.'

When I imagine Jesus walking over to me and asking me the same question, I struggle with what my request would be. Yes, I have bills that are crippling me. But I'm not sure that 'pay my bills' would be the answer I would give – it would mean only temporary relief.

After much thought and prayer, I believe I have my answer, revealed to me by the Holy Spirit. The funny thing is that the answer was there in scripture the whole time. As I continued praying, I gave my answer to Jesus: 'Lord, let my eyes be opened.'

I remembered how often I have asked Jesus to open my eyes that I may see God's mysteries, to open my ears to hear and to open my mind to perceive truthfully. This precious gift from Jesus draws me closer to God.

Prayer: *Dear Jesus, thank you for answered prayers. Thank you for having mercy on us and for bringing us into relationship with you. Amen*

Thought for the day: What do I want Jesus to do for me?

Jabulile Gubula (Gauteng, South Africa)

Ageing with grace

Read Micah 6:6–8

[God] has told you, O mortal, what is good; and what does the Lord require of you but to do justice, and to love kindness, and to walk humbly with your God?

Micah 6:8 (NRSV)

Recently I turned 73. During the previous year, I had begun to feel life changing. My body was ageing – my strength, energy and endurance were lessening. I had to give up driving at night. I needed hearing aids and I struggled with arthritis.

Having spent my life seeking to do things for others, I resented these limits on my actions and activities. Grieving and embarrassed that I couldn't do all that I used to do, I wondered, 'What good am I at this stage of life? What is my mission now?'

I discovered answers in Micah 6:8 – words that teach me how to accept ageing with humility and grace. They restore to me mission and purpose, telling me that I don't have to do great deeds to make a difference. So these days my mission and its impact are clear. Every time I pray for justice to reign, every act of mercy I show, and each time I choose to put another ahead of myself, the world shifts a tiny bit for the good – and God is pleased.

Prayer: *Creator God, when we doubt our purpose, renew our vision. Help us to be faithful, humble servants, doing what we can to make this world a better place. Amen*

Thought for the day: God values every small act of service, even those I deem insignificant.

Virginia Jelinek (Pennsylvania, US)

Small group questions

Wednesday 1 January

1 What New Year's traditions does your family observe? What do these traditions mean to you, and how do they shape your view of this time of year?

2 Describe a time recently when you were reminded of your human mortality. What gives you consolation when you consider your own mortality?

3 What signs of God's grace come to mind when you think about your life? What spiritual practices make you more aware of God's grace in your life? What new practice would you like to try this year to help you recognise God's grace?

4 Which scripture passage most reminds you of the passing of time? Does the scripture passage bring you comfort or cause you to worry? Why do you think you respond to it in this way?

5 Today's writer expresses gratitude for his lively Christian congregation. For which qualities of your faith community are you most thankful?

Wednesday 8 January

1 How would you respond to the question, 'Who are you?' Do you find that you are often quick to share your identity as a child of God? Why or why not?

2 Describe a time when someone enriched your faith like the student in today's meditation enriched the writer's faith. What kind of lasting impact has that made on your life? Name some ways you can enrich the faith of others.

3 Does knowing that you are a child of God affect your relationship with him? Why or why not? How do you strengthen and deepen your relationship with God?

4   What practices help you to be more aware of your faith? What do you do to encourage others to join the family of God?

5   How does your church help you to remain grounded in your identity as a child of God? What changes would you like to see in how your church emphasises this identity?

Wednesday 15 January

1   Do you find it hard to make time for prayer? Have you tried a method similar to the one today's writer uses, or do you have another method you prefer? Describe your experience with making more time to pray.

2   Which scripture verses help you understand the importance of prayer? Which scripture passages have inspired you to try a new form of prayer?

3   Does being with nature inspire you to pray? What other times, events or locations most inspire you to pray? Why?

4   Today's writer encouraged his friend to make time for prayer. Describe a time when you have encouraged someone to strengthen their spiritual life. How did that experience affect you and the person you encouraged?

5   How does your church pray? Is prayer reserved for worship? How do you think your church community would be different if everyone made more time for prayer?

Wednesday 22 January

1   When have you felt closest to God? What led to that feeling of close-ness? Do you think spending more time with God and reading the Bible brings us closer to him? Why or why not?

2   Describe someone who you think spends a significant amount of time with God each day. What do they do? How does their faith inspire you in your own spiritual practice?

3   The writer talks about the importance of allowing God to carry us. What does it mean to you to let God carry you? Describe a time when you allowed him to carry you. How has that experience increased your reliance on him?

4   When has someone in your church community carried you? How does it look different to allow God to carry us rather than other Christians?

5   What kinds of community outreach does your church engage in? In what ways do these ministries bring people closer to God? In what other ways can you provide care for those in your community and show them God's love?

Wednesday 29 January

1   What do you think Jesus was trying to convey in the two parables in today's reading?

2   What things have you learned from the Bible that have changed you? Do you search for such instruction or do you feel you are guided towards them?

3   Have you ever felt that God has asked you to make changes in your life that are difficult? If so, how did you react?

4   Does some teaching found in the Bible take a long time to assimilate? Why do you think this is?

5   What things can we do to ensure that we grow in our faith? How would you put these ideas into action?

Wednesday 5 February

1   Describe a time when you experienced a loss. How did others who were suffering help you? What difference did it make?

2   Have you ever thought about the parable of the good Samaritan from the same perspective as today's writer? If not, does his perspective make you react differently to the parable? Describe how the parable reminds and encourages you to show love to others.

3 Who are your 'neighbours' today? What are the most effective ways you can show them love?

4 Today's writer says that showing compassion is one way we imitate Christ. In what other ways do you think we can imitate Christ and draw closer to God and those around us?

5 Where do you see your community reaching out in compassion to others? Do you participate? If so, what have you learned from your experience? If not, how can you get involved?

Wednesday 12 February

1 Would you describe yourself as a curious person? Who is the most curious person you know? What are some of the benefits of being curious? In what areas would you like to cultivate your sense of curiosity?

2 What role does your history play in who you are today? How do you honour your history and the traditions of your family?

3 What traditions do you hope to continue to pass down in your family? In your community? Globally? Why are these traditions important to you?

4 Have you taken time to study the history of the church and its traditions? If so, in what ways does that information change the way you view the church? If not, what are some ways you can learn more about your church tradition?

5 What church traditions do you think transcend denominational boundaries? How do traditions bring us closer together?

Wednesday 19 February

1 How do you focus on sharing your faith with others? Which scripture verses remind you of the importance of sharing your faith?

2 When have you criticised someone or dismissed their efforts? How did they respond? What practices help you to avoid criticising others?

3   Describe a time when you witnessed God working through human efforts to reach others. What was the outcome? How does this situation encourage you in your own efforts?

4   Do you sometimes question the efficacy of other people's methods of evangelising? Do you think it is okay to question others in this way? Why or why not?

5   Is it easy or difficult for you to remain open to the ways God has called you to share your faith? How do you remain willing to follow the call? What do you do if you don't like what you are called to do?

Wednesday February 26

1   Today's writer uses sea glass to remind us that God sees each of us as unique and beautiful? What other things remind you that God sees value in all of us? How do these reminders bring you comfort?

2   Describe a time when you felt discarded, broken or unworthy of God's love. How did you remember your value? What people, prayers, spiritual practices, scripture passages or objects helped you to remember?

3   How can we remain open to God's transformation in us? Do you think we are ever finished being transformed, or is God continually working on us? Give some examples.

4   Name someone you know who doesn't seem to realise their value. What will you do to help them and show them God's love?

5   Describe what you see when you think of the church as a whole. Is it a colourful mosaic of sea glass or do you see something else? How does the way you think of the church as a whole affect the way you feel about it?

Wednesday 4 March

1   Describe a time in your life when you struggled to understand God's timing. How was your faith changed by this experience?

2 Today's writer talks about how Joseph had to wait on God's timing. What other biblical characters had to wait to see God's ultimate plan for them? With which character do you identify most? Why?

3 How do you react when you're struggling to trust God's timing? What spiritual practices bring you peace during such times?

4 What can you do to help someone who is struggling to wait for God? How can your church support those who are struggling?

5 What situations do you see in your life or in the lives of others that remind you that God is always at work?

Wednesday 11 March

1 What dead branches do you have in your life? What practices can help you trim them from your life? How do you hope this will change the ways you serve God?

2 Describe a time when you felt the Holy Spirit nudging you to make a change in your life. Did you make the change? If not, what held you back?

3 In what ways do you produce fruit for God's kingdom? In what new ways would you like to produce fruit? What kind of support from your church community would make this easier?

4 Do you find it difficult to prune away negative behaviour or patterns in your life? If so, why? If not, what makes it easy for you?

5 Do other Christians in your community serve as examples of faith for you? What qualities do you admire in them? How can their examples help you in your own faith experience?

Wednesday 18 March

1 When have you struggled with unbelief? How did you overcome your doubt? How can unbelief be an ongoing struggle?

2 Several biblical characters struggle with doubt and unbelief. Name the ones that stand out to you most. What is memorable about these characters? How do they respond to and work through their doubts?

3 Where do you find the most reassurance from God? In scripture, through prayer, in nature, among other Christians or elsewhere? Talk about why you find reassurance in these places.

4 Do you find it easy or difficult to ask God for help when you experience doubt? Why? What prayers or spiritual practices help to strengthen your faith?

5 What does it mean to you that God's goodness will cover your weakness? Do you find comfort in that knowledge? How do you see Jesus' goodness making up for the areas of your life where you may be weak?

Wednesday 25 March

1 Who in your life clearly demonstrates the strength of their faith? How do they do so? In what ways would you like to follow their example?

2 Has someone you know experienced a great loss recently? Name some ways you can help both physically and spiritually during this time.

3 Is it easy or difficult for you to remain cheerful towards and thoughtful of others when you are going through hard times? Why? Where do you find peace and resilience during such times?

4 In what ways do others show kindness to you? In what ways do you show kindness to others? How can you be more intentional about showing kindness and love to those around you?

5 At times, do you find yourself clinging to earthly possessions? What spiritual practices help you to shift your focus back to Christ? Which scripture verses help you?

Wednesday 1 April

1 Recall a time when you did not feel qualified for what God was calling you to do. How did you respond? Where did you find strength and reassurance?

2 When have you felt abandoned by God? Why did you feel that way?

What helped you realise that God had not abandoned you? What reminds you that he is always with you?

3 What does it look like to be an 'ambassador for Christ' and to carry out the ministry of reconciliation? Do you ever feel unworthy of that task? How do you persevere through those feelings?

4 How do you currently serve God? How does Christ's presence in your life help you accomplish this work? What scripture verses remind you that you are qualified to serve God?

5 In what ways can you encourage others who feel unworthy to serve God? How could your church better support its members in their service to him?

Wednesday 8 April

1 Do you find it difficult to forgive others? If not, what makes it easy for you to forgive? If so, why? How does Jesus' example help you to forgive? What practical steps can you take to help you forgive more freely?

2 Describe a time when you felt a desire for revenge. Did you act on that desire? If so, what was the outcome of the situation? If you didn't seek revenge, who or what helped you make peace with the situation?

3 Besides Jesus, which other biblical characters serve as examples of forgiveness for you? What have you learned from them?

4 What does it mean to see the world through God's eyes? How do you reflect his love and forgiveness in your daily life?

5 What would your life be like if you offered understanding and forgiveness as freely as Jesus did? What would your community be like if others did the same? How would the world be changed if everyone offered that forgiveness to others?

Wednesday 15 April

1 Do you have many scars? What memories or feelings do you have when you see your scars? How might you learn to see your scars as signs of healing and view them in a positive way?

2 What songs, poems or scripture passages comfort you when you are going through a challenging situation? Describe a time when something you heard or read helped you to better understand your healing process. How did it help you?

3 Recall a time when you witnessed God's power to restore and transform your life or the life of someone you know. How does that situation encourage you today?

4 How does knowing that Jesus experienced suffering change the way you think about God? Does it help you to face challenges with more hope? Do you struggle to understand such suffering? How do you make peace with difficult experiences?

5 What encouragement would you offer to someone who has many scars? How can you show them God's love?

Wednesday 22 April

1 Do you ever think about God as giving us favours for our good behaviour? What has shaped your understanding of God? How does that affect the way you live?

2 What does scripture say about the way God views our behaviour? Point to specific passages that support what you say.

3 Have you ever felt like Joshua did when you see God working through someone who does not seem to be following God's will? What did you learn from the experience?

4 In what ways do you find it meaningful to know that God's love for us is not dependent on our behaviour? Is there anything that we can do to separate ourselves from God's love forever? How do you remain faithful during times when you feel tempted to ignore God's will?

5 How does your church help you to remember that God's love is not dependent upon us or our behaviour? Who serves as an example of being open to God's purpose in their life? How does this person's example help you in your own faith journey?

Wednesday 29 April

1 What do you want Jesus to do for you? Have you ever felt guilty about asking him for something? Why did you feel guilty?

2 Do you find it easy to get caught up in temporary concerns such as those the author mentions? How do you regain focus on things that have more long-lasting consequences?

3 What does it mean to live with open eyes, ears and minds? How do you know whether you're open to God and to others? What spiritual practices help you remain open to God?

4 What scripture passages remind you to ask God for what you want and need? Which Bible verses help you see areas in your life where you could strengthen your faith and your relationship with God?

5 How does living with eyes, ears and mind open change the way you interact with those in your community? What needs in your community could you provide for? In what ways would you like to better serve those around you? How will you strengthen your relationships with your neighbours?

Journal page

At this time of Lent, David Walker explores different aspects of human belonging through the medium of scripture and story, in order to help us recognise the different ways in which we are God's beloved. And as we recognise ourselves and our own lives in the narrative of God's engagement with humanity and his creation, he gently challenges us to engage for God's sake with God's world.

You Are Mine
Daily Bible readings from Ash Wednesday to Easter Day
David Walker
978 0 85746 758 4   £8.99
brfonline.org.uk

Journeying through Lent
with **New Daylight**

Daily Bible readings
and group study material

Eight weeks of Lent material for church groups and individuals, offering themed reflections by well-loved contributors from the *New Daylight* archive alongside specially written questions for group discussion. Weeks 1 and 2: Feasting and fasting – Helen Julian CSF; Weeks 3 and 4: The sermon on the mount – Rachel Boulding; Weeks 5 and 6: Jesus' wisdom in Luke – Stephen Cottrell; Week 7: 1 Corinthians 13 – Tony Horsfall; Week 8: From upper room to Easter Day – Brother Ramon.

Journeying through Lent with New Daylight
Daily Bible readings and group study material
978 0 85746 965 6 £2.99
brfonline.org.uk

How to read the Bible? And how to apply it? To read and engage with the Bible, we first need to understand the story, the styles of writing and the approaches we find in the text. Michael Parsons encourages readers to look at the whole biblical storyline before demonstrating ways of approaching individual texts. Topics along the way include understanding different genres, the importance of narrative, imaginative reading, praying the Bible, difficult passages and what to do with them, and how to apply scripture to our own lives.

How to Read the Bible
... so that it makes a difference
Michael Parsons
978 0 85746 809 3 £8.99
brfonline.org.uk

The life stories of the Celtic saints are inspirational. They demonstrate great and unassuming faith, often in the face of insurmountable difficulties. In *Celtic Saints* David Cole draws us to relate our own life journey and developing relationship with God into the life story of the Celtic saint of the day. A corresponding biblical text and blessing encourages and motivates us to transform our lives for today's world in the light of such historic faith.

Celtic Saints
40 days of devotional readings
David Cole
978 0 85746 950 2 £8.99
brfonline.org.uk

I would like to make a gift to support BRF. Please use my gift for:

☐ where it is needed most ☐ Barnabas in Schools ☐ Parenting for Faith

☐ Messy Church ☐ Anna Chaplaincy

Title	First name/initials	Surname

Address

Postcode

Email

Telephone

Signature	Date

giftaid it You can add an extra 25p to every £1 you give.

Please treat as Gift Aid donations all qualifying gifts of money made

☐ today, ☐ in the past four years, ☐ and in the future.

I am a UK taxpayer and understand that if I pay less Income Tax and/or Capital Gains Tax in the current tax year than the amount of Gift Aid claimed on all my donations, it is my responsibility to pay any difference.

☐ My donation does not qualify for Gift Aid.

Please notify BRF if you want to cancel this Gift Aid declaration, change your name or home address, or no longer pay sufficient tax on your income and/or capital gains.

Please complete other side of form ➡

Please return this form to:

BRF, 15 The Chambers, Vineyard, Abingdon OX14 3FE

The Bible Reading Fellowship is a Registered Charity (233280)

SHARING OUR VISION – MAKING A GIFT

Regular giving

By Direct Debit: You can set up a Direct Debit quickly and easily at **brf.org.uk/donate**

By Standing Order: Please contact our Fundraising Administrator +44 (0)1865 319700 | **giving@brf.org.uk**

One-off donation

Please accept my gift of:

☐ £10 ☐ £50 ☐ £100 Other £ ☐

by (*delete as appropriate*):

☐ Cheque/Charity Voucher payable to 'BRF'

☐ MasterCard/Visa/Debit card/Charity card

Name on card

Card no. ☐☐☐☐ ☐☐☐☐ ☐☐☐☐ ☐☐☐☐

Expires end ☐M☐M ☐Y☐Y Security code* ☐☐☐

*Last 3 digits on the reverse of the card
ESSENTIAL IN ORDER TO PROCESS
YOUR PAYMENT

Signature   Date

☐ I would like to leave a gift in my will to BRF.

For more information, visit **brf.org.uk/lastingdifference**

For help or advice regarding making a gift, please contact our Fundraising Administrator +44 (0)1865 319700

↰ Please complete other side of form

Please return this form to:
BRF, 15 The Chambers, Vineyard, Abingdon OX14 3FE

The Bible Reading Fellowship is a Registered Charity (233280)

UR0120

How to encourage Bible reading in your church

BRF has been helping individuals connect with the Bible for over 90 years. We want to support churches as they seek to encourage church members into regular Bible reading.

Order a Bible reading resources pack
This pack is designed to give your church the tools to publicise our Bible reading notes. It includes:

- Sample Bible reading notes for your congregation to try.
- Publicity resources, including a poster.
- A church magazine feature about Bible reading notes.

The pack is free, but we welcome a £5 donation to cover the cost of postage. If you require a pack to be sent outside the UK or require a specific number of sample Bible reading notes, please contact us for postage costs. More information about what the current pack contains is available on our website.

How to order and find out more
- Visit **biblereadingnotes.org.uk/for-churches**.
- Telephone BRF on +44 (0)1865 319700 Mon–Fri 9.15–17.30.
- Write to us at BRF, 15 The Chambers, Vineyard, Abingdon OX14 3FE.

Keep informed about our latest initiatives
We are continuing to develop resources to help churches encourage people into regular Bible reading, wherever they are on their journey. Join our email list at **brfonline.org.uk/signup** to stay informed about the latest initiatives that your church could benefit from.

Subscriptions

The Upper Room is published in January, May and September.

Individual subscriptions
The subscription rate for orders for 4 or fewer copies includes postage and packing:

The Upper Room annual individual subscription   £17.40

Group subscriptions
Orders for 5 copies or more, sent to ONE address, are post free:
The Upper Room annual group subscription   £13.80

Please do not send payment with order for a group subscription. We will send an invoice with your first order.

Please note that the annual billing period for group subscriptions runs from 1 May to 30 April.

Copies of the notes may also be obtained from Christian bookshops.

Single copies of *The Upper Room* cost £4.60.

Prices valid until 30 April 2020.

Giant print version
The Upper Room is available in giant print for the visually impaired, from:

Torch Trust for the Blind
Torch House
Torch Way
Northampton Road
Market Harborough
LE16 9HL

Tel: +44 (0)1858 438260
torchtrust.org

All our Bible reading notes can be ordered online by visiting biblereadingnotes.org.uk/subscriptions

☐ I would like to take out a subscription myself (complete your name and address details once)

☐ I would like to give a gift subscription (please provide both names and addresses)

Title .... First name/initials .... Surname ....

Address ....

.... Postcode ....

Telephone .... Email ....

Gift subscription name ....

Gift subscription address ....

.... Postcode ....

Gift message (20 words max. or include your own gift card):

....

....

Please send *The Upper Room* beginning with the May 2020 / September 2020 / January 2021 issue (*delete as appropriate*):

Annual individual subscription ☐ £17.40   Total enclosed £ ....

Method of payment

☐ Cheque (made payable to BRF)   ☐ MasterCard / Visa

Card no. ☐☐☐☐ ☐☐☐☐ ☐☐☐☐ ☐☐☐☐

Expires end ☐☐ M M ☐☐ Y Y   Security code* ☐☐☐   Last 3 digits on the reverse of the card

*ESSENTIAL IN ORDER TO PROCESS THE PAYMENT

THE UPPER ROOM GROUP SUBSCRIPTION FORM

> **All our Bible reading notes can be ordered online by visiting biblereadingnotes.org.uk/subscriptions**

☐ Please send me .... copies of *The Upper Room* May 2020 / September 2020 / January 2021 issue (*delete as appropriate*)

Title .... First name/initials .... Surname ....

Address ....

.... Postcode ....

Telephone .... Email ....

Please do not send payment with this order. We will send an invoice with your first order.

Christian bookshops: All good Christian bookshops stock BRF publications. For your nearest stockist, please contact BRF.

Telephone: The BRF office is open Mon–Fri 9.15–17.30. To place your order, telephone +44 (0)1865 319700.

Online: biblereadingnotes.org.uk/group-subscriptions

☐ Please send me a Bible reading resources pack to encourage Bible reading in my church

Please return this form with the appropriate payment to:
BRF, 15 The Chambers, Vineyard, Abingdon OX14 3FE
To read our terms and find out about cancelling your order, please visit **brfonline.org.uk/terms**.

The Bible Reading Fellowship is a Registered Charity (233280)

UR0120

To order

Delivery times within the UK are normally 15 working days. Prices are correct at the time of going to press but may change without prior notice.

Title	Price	Qty	Total
You Are Mine	£8.99		
Journeying through Lent with New Daylight	£2.99		
How to Read the Bible	£8.99		
Celtic Saints	£8.99		

POSTAGE AND PACKING CHARGES			
Order value	UK	Europe	Rest of world
Under £7.00	£2.00		
£7.00–£29.99	£3.00	Available on request	Available on request
£30.00 and over	FREE		

Total value of books	
Postage and packing	
Donation	
Total for this order	

Please complete in BLOCK CAPITALS

Title .... First name/initials .... Surname..................................

Address ....

.... Postcode ....

Acc. No. .... Telephone ....

Email ....

Method of payment

❏ Cheque (made payable to BRF) ❏ MasterCard / Visa

Card no. ☐☐☐☐ ☐☐☐☐ ☐☐☐☐ ☐☐☐☐ ☐☐☐☐ ☐☐☐☐

Expires end ☐M☐M ☐Y☐Y Security code* ☐☐☐ Last 3 digits on the reverse of the card

Signature* .... Date ..../........../..........
*ESSENTIAL IN ORDER TO PROCESS YOUR ORDER

The Bible Reading Fellowship Gift Aid Declaration

giftaid it

Please treat as Gift Aid donations all qualifying gifts of money made

❏ today, ❏ in the past four years, ❏ and in the future **or** ❏ My donation does not qualify for Gift Aid.

I am a UK taxpayer and understand that if I pay less Income Tax and/or Capital Gains Tax in the current tax year than the amount of Gift Aid claimed on all my donations, it is my responsibility to pay any difference.

Please notify BRF if you want to cancel this declaration, change your name or home address, or no longer pay sufficient tax on your income and/or capital gains.

Please return this form to: BRF, 15 The Chambers, Vineyard, Abingdon OX14 3FE | enquiries@brf.org.uk
To read our terms and find out about cancelling your order, please visit **brfonline.org.uk/terms**.

The Bible Reading Fellowship (BRF) is a Registered Charity (233280)